COUNTRY

CELLAR

COMPILED BY:

RUTH BLACKETT

BONNIE MILLHOLLIN

EDITED BY:

KATHEY SHREVES

ILLUSTRATIONS BY:

KAREN WALKER

OTHER COOKBOOKS AVAILABLE:

ZUCCHINI PATCH
BERRY PATCH
APPLE CELLAR

PRINTED BY:

CROWN PRINTERS
122 NO. RUSSELL
SANTA MARIA, CA   93454

1981

COPIES MAY BE ORDERED FROM:

ZUCCHINI PATCH
P.O. BOX 1100
NIPOMO, CA   93444
(805) 929-1718

Our grateful appreciation to those who contributed
to the compilation of this book:

Lisa Bailey

Pam Cespedes

Bonnie and Ken Corcoran

Kebben and Melody Kortness

Marian and Dick Marangi

Ivan C. Millhollin

Karen Milo

Niki Reese

Heather Jo Shreves

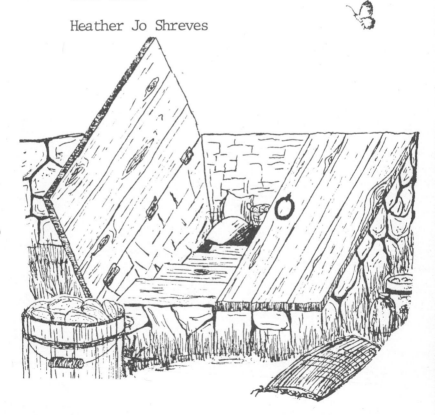

TABLE OF CONTENTS

APPETIZERS

LADY LUCK SAVORY DIP

½ cup shredded carrots
4 slices bacon, diced
1 cup (8 ounce) sour cream
2 tablespoons chutney, finely chopped
¼ teaspoon curry powder
  Dash bottled red pepper sauce
3 tablespoons chopped green onions

In small skillet cook bacon until crisp; drain well.
In small bowl combine sour cream, chutney, curry powder
and pepper sauce until well mixed. Fold in bacon,
carrots and green onions. Cover and refrigerate
at least 1 to 2 hours before serving. Makes about
1¼ cups.

POTATOES CON QUESO

¼ cup butter or margarine
½ cup finely chopped onion
1 can (1 lb.) tomatoes, undrained
1½ to 2 cans (4 ounce) green chiles, drained
  and chopped
½ teaspoon salt
1 lb Monterey Jack cheese, cubed
½ cup heavy cream
3 medium potatoes

Boil potatoes in jackets. Do not overcook, as
they must be firm. Cool potatoes. Peel and cut
into small cubes. Set aside. In melted butter,
saute onion until tender. Add tomatoes, chiles
and salt, mashing tomatoes with a fork. Simmer,
stirring occasionally, 15 minutes. Add cheese
cubes, stirring until cheese is melted. Stir
in cream. Cook, stirring constantly, 2 minutes.
Remove from heat, and let stand 15 minutes.
Pour into casserole over a candle warmer. Dip
potatoe cubes (using toothpicks) into mixture.
Makes 10 to 12 servings.

SHRIMP-VEGETABLE TEMPURA

1 pound shrimps, shelled and cleaned
12 small green onions, cut in 3-inch lengths
2 medium carrots, cut in ½-inch thick, 3-inch
    long sticks
2 medium red or green peppers, cut in ½-inch wide
    3-inch long strips
½ pound whole green beans, ends trimmed
½ pound small cauliflorets
    Oil for deep-fat frying

Batter:
2 eggs, well beaten
1 cup water
1 cup flour
1 tablespoon cornstarch
½ teaspoon each, baking powder and salt

Sauce:
½ cup soy sauce
3 tablespoons vinegar
1 teaspoon sugar
1 teaspoon grated fresh ginger

Dry shrimps and vegetables with paper towels. Heat
oil in pan to 375°. Meanwhile in small bowl mix
batter ingredients; set aside. Mix sauce ingredients
in small saucepan; heat through; keep warm. Drop
several pieces in batter; lift out with tongs or
slotted spoon. Allow to drain before placing in oil
in pan. Cook until lightly browned. Drain; serve
hot with sauce for dipping. Makes 8 servings.

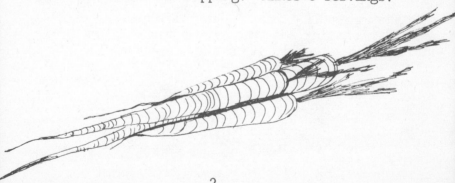

CARROTS IN CHEESE

1 package (3 ounces) cream cheese
½ teaspoon Worcestershire
    cream
16 1-inch thick carrot slices
¼ pound salted almonds, chopped fine

Mix cheese and Worcestershire together with
enough cream to make a thick paste. Coat
carrots with mixture; roll in almonds. Chill.
Makes 16.

TERRIYAKI MEATBALLS

1 tablespoon soy sauce
1 tablespoon water
2 teaspoons sugar
¼ teaspoon instant minced onion
    dash garlic salt
    dash monosodium glutamate
    dash ground ginger
½ pound lean ground beef
½ cup grated potatoes
    salad oil

Combine soy sauce, water, sugar, onion, garlic
salt, monosodium glutamate, and ginger; let
stand 10 minutes. Combine ground beef and
grated potatoes; stir in soy mixture. Shape
into 3/4-inch meatballs. Spear meatballs on
bamboo skewers; cook in deep hot fat in a
fondue pot about 1½ minutes. Makes about 2½
dozen balls.

CREAMY CLAM GUACAMOLE

½ cup grated carrots
¼ cup dairy sour cream
2 tablespoons lemon juice
1 teaspoon chopped onions
1 teaspoon salt, ½ teaspoon hot pepper sauce
2 ripe avocados, peeled and quartered
1 can (7½ ounces) minced clams, drained

In blender, at low speed, blend all ingredients
except clams. Stir in clams. Spoon mixture into
serving bowl; cover and refrigerate several hours
to blend flavors. Serve dip surrounded by Hot
Tater Tots or potatoe chips. Makes 2 cups.

JAZZY BEEF BITES

1 tablespoon catsup
1 teaspoon prepared horseradish
1 teaspoon prepared mustard
½ teaspoon instant minced onion
½ teaspoon salt
   dash pepper
1 egg
½ cup grated carrots
½ pound lean ground beef
¼ cup fine soft bread crumbs
   Sharp natural Cheddar cheese, cut in ¼-inch
   cubes
   Salad oil

Combine first 8 ingredients; let stand 10 minutes.
Combine ground beef and bread crumbs; stir in
catsup mixture. Shape meat around cheese cubes
into 3/4-inch meatballs. Spear meatballs on
bamboo skewers; cook in deep hot fat in fondue
pot about 1½ minutes or bake in oven at 375°
for 10 minutes. Makes about 2½ dozen balls.

SWEET AND SOUR PORK

1 pound lean pork, cut into ½-inch pieces
2 tablespoons cooking oil
  salt and pepper to taste
1 cup beef bouillon
2 carrots, sliced thin
1 large green pepper, slivered
1 small onion, thinly sliced
2½ cups pineapple chunks, drained
¼ cup sugar
½ cup pineapple syrup
¼ cup vinegar
3 tablespoons cornstarch
2 teaspoons soy sauce
  Hot cooked rice

Brown pork in hot oil. Season. Add bouillon.
Simmer, covered, for 30 minutes. Add vegetables
and pineapple. Blend together remaining
ingredients and add to mixture. Cook, stirring
frequently, for 10 minutes. Serve with toothpicks.
Makes 8-10 servings.

TUCSON SWEETS

1½ cups mashed cooked yams
1 beaten egg
½ cup finely chopped dates
2 tablespoons butter
  pinch of cinnamon
  salt to taste
  nuts

Combine all ingredients except nuts, chill and
shape into tiny balls. Roll in finely chopped
nuts. Bake on a greased baking sheet at 375°
for 10-15 minutes.

COTTAGE CHEESE SPREAD

Top toast rounds with cottage cheese mixed with crumbled crisp bacon and shredded carrots. Garnish with slice of stuffed olive.

CARROT AND PEANUT-BUTTER SANDWICHES

Grate raw carrots fine to make ½ cup. Stir into 1 cup crunchy-style peanut butter. Use immediately. Spread on melba toast rounds.

CARROT CHEESE STRATA

   8 slices day old bread
   8 ounces sharp natural Cheddar cheese, sliced
   4 eggs
2½ cups milk
   1 tablespoon minced onion
1½ teaspoon salt
   ½ teaspoon dry mustard
   1 cup grated carrots

Trim crusts from 5 slices of the bread; cut in half diagonally. Use trimmings and remaining 3 slices untrimmed bread to cover bottom of 8 or 9 inch square baking dish. Top with cheese. Arrange the 10 trimmed "triangles" in two rows atop the cheese. Beat eggs; blend in milk, onion, salt, dash pepper, mustard and grated carrots. Pour over bread and cheese. Cover with waxed paper; let stand 1 hour at room temperature or several hours in refrigerator. Bake in slow oven (325º) for 1 hour or until knife inserted comes out clean. Let stand for 5 minutes before serving. Cut in bite size squares.

POTATO QUICHE IDAHO

4 potatoes
1 egg
1 teaspoon salt
¼ teaspoon white pepper or dash hot-pepper sauce
½ teaspoon ground nutmeg

Scrub potatoes. Dry. Prick with a fork. Bake
in 425° oven 45 to 50 minutes until tender.
Remove from oven and leave oven on. Cut potatoes
in half. Scoop out pulp and place in medium-size
bowl. Mash potatoes well. Add egg, salt, pepper
and nutmeg; mix well. Press potato mixture into
a deep 9½-inch pie plate. Prick with a fork.
Bake in 425° oven 12 minutes. Remove and cool
slightly. Reduce oven temperature to 325°.

QUICHE FILLING

2 tablespoons butter or margarine
¼ pound fresh mushrooms, sliced
1 small red pepper, seeded and chopped
¼ pound Swiss cheese, diced
5 eggs
2 cups skim milk
1 teaspoon salt
1 teaspoon pepper
½ teaspoon ground nutmeg

In small skillet, melt butter; saute mushrooms
and red pepper until tender. Arrange sauteed
vegetables and cheese in pie shell. In medium
size bowl, beat together eggs, milk, salt, pepper
and nutmeg; pour mixture into pie shell. Bake
in 325° oven 30 minutes or until filling is set.
Allow to cool 15 minutes before serving. Cut
into thin wedges.

VEGETABLE DIP

¼ cup light cream
2 cups creamed cottage cheese
¼ cup minced raw carrots
¼ cup thinly sliced scallions
8 radishes, sliced very thinly
½ teaspoon salt
¼ teaspoon pepper

Combine all ingredients and chill before serving.
Makes about 2-3/4 cups.

CURRIED TURKEY SPREAD

1 package (8 ounce) cream cheese, softened
½ cup grated carrots
1 cup chopped toasted almonds
½ cup mayonnaise
2 tablespoons chutney, chopped
1 tablespoon curry powder
¼ teaspoon salt
  Minced parsley or chopped toasted almonds for garnish

Mix well all ingredients except garnish. Shape into
ball, wrap airtight and chill or freeze. Before
serving, roll in parsley. Serve as an appetizer
with crackers or sliced celery, zucchini or
cucumber. Makes 12 to 16 servings.

CARROT AND ONION TEA SANDWICHES

Grate raw carrots fine. Add a small amount of
scraped onion and mayonnaise to moisten. Season
to taste. Spread on small bread triangles.

POTATO PIROSHKIS

Prepare pie crust for single crust pie. Roll out
dough to a thickness of 1/16 to 1/8 inch. Cut out
2-inch circles, using a cookie cutter or the rim
of a glass dipped in flour. Place a rounded
teaspoonful of potatoe and cheese filling on one
half of each circle. Fold over other half, and
pinch edges together with tines of a fork.
Brush surface of pastries with beaten egg yolk.
Bake in 400° oven 20 to 25 minutes, until golden
brown. Makes 18.

POTATO AND CHEESE FILLING

In a small saucepan, combine 6 tablespoons milk,
1 tablespoon finely chopped onion, and 1 tablespoon
butter or margarine. Heat until milk just begins
to boil; remove from heat. Using a fork, gradually
stir in 3 tablespoons instant mashed-potatoes mix.
Add ½ cup cottage cheese, ¼ teaspoon salt, dash
ground nutmeg, and dash of pepper. Cool slightly
and stir in one beaten egg.

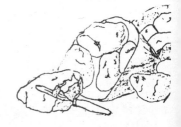

MUSHROOMS ALA KAREN

12 large mushrooms
 1 cup mashed potatoes
 ½ cup sharp Cheddar cheese
 ¼ cup finely chopped ham
 ¼ cup finely chopped green onion

Remove mushroom stems. Mix potatoes, cheese, ham
and green onions. Fill mushroom caps with mixture.
Place in shallow baking dish. Bake in preheated
oven (325°) for about 25 minutes. Makes 12 servings.

MARINATED MUSHROOM ANTIPASTO

DRESSING

1 cup white vinegar
½ cup olive oil
¼ cup finely chopped onion
2 cloves garlic, crushed
1 teaspoon salt, 1 teaspoon sugar
1 teaspoon dried basil leaves
1 teaspoon dried oregano leaves
¼ teaspoon pepper

½ pound mushrooms, washed and sliced ¼-inch thick
1 can (14 ounce) artichoke hearts, drained and
    cut in half lengthwise
1 can (7¼ ounce) baby carrots, drained
¼ cup coursely chopped pimiento
1 cup pitted black olives

Mix all dressing ingredients in saucepan. Bring
to boil, over medium heat. Remove from heat;
cool 10 minutes. Meanwhile, in medium mixing
bowl, layer all vegetables, starting with mushrooms
and ending with olives. Pour cooled dressing
over vegetables. Refrigerate, covered, several
hours or overnight. Before serving, toss gently
to mix well. Makes 1 quart.

POTATOES MAYONNAISE

3 medium potatoes
2 tablespoons dairy sour cream
½ cup mayonnaise
    dash of curry
    salt and pepper to taste

Boil potatoes in jackets. Do not overcook, as
they must not be mushy. Cool potatoes. Peel
and cut into small cubes. Mix remaining
ingredients. Carefully coat cubes with mixture.
Serve with toothpicks. Makes 3 to 4 dozen.

CARROT PATE

1½ pounds carrots, cut in 2-inch pieces
   salt
 3 eggs
½ cup mayonnaise
2 teaspoons Worcestershire
1 teaspoon white vinegar
½ teaspoon each, salt and thyme
   dash hot-pepper sauce
1 teaspoon dried parsley flakes

Grease 7½x4x2-inch loaf pan; line with waxed
paper; grease again; set aside. Cook carrots
covered in lightly salted boiling water about
10 minutes (do not overcook). In blender, whirl
eggs, mayonnaise and seasonings until well blended,
then add carrots and whirl until carrots are ground
coarse. Spoon mixture into prepared pan. Place
in pan with 1 inch hot water. Bake in preheated
375° oven 35 to 40 minutes or until knife inserted
in center comes out clean. Remove from water;
cool on rack 10 minutes. Loosen around edges and
unmold on serving dish. Sprinkle with parsley.
Slice and serve warm or chilled. Makes 15 slices.

HOT SAUSAGE AND CHEESE PUFFS

1 pound hot or sweet Italian sausage
1 pound sharp Cheddar cheese, shredded
3 cups biscuit baking mix
1 cup water
1 cup grated carrots

Remove sausage from casings; cook in large skillet,
about 8 to 10 minutes. Drain off fat, cook completely.
Add cheese, biscuit mix and water; mix with a fork
just until blended. Roll into 1-inch balls; place
on large cookie sheets 2 inches apart. Bake in
hot oven (400°) for 12 to 15 minutes or until
puffed and browned. Remove from cookie sheets;
cool completely on wire racks.

WALNUT DUXELLE PUFFS

4 cups finely chopped mushrooms
1 cup grated carrots
½ cup chopped green onion
¼ teaspoon powdered thyme
1 tablespoon butter or margarine
½ teaspoon salt
½ cup dry sherry
1 (8 ounce) package cream cheese
1 cup chopped toasted walnuts
¼ cup chopped parsley

Cook mushrooms, carrots, onion and thyme with butter until onion is transparent, stirring frequently. Add salt and sherry and cook until liquid is almost completely evaporated. Remove from heat and cool. Soften cream cheese and mix with mushroom mixture. Just before serving, blend in walnuts and parsley. Serve as a spread with a variety of crackers.

FRENCH MUSHROOMS

12 large mushrooms
 3 slices bacon
·1 onion, chopped fine
¼ cup chopped green pepper
1 cup mashed potatoes
2 tablespoons chopped parsley
½ teaspoon seasoned salt

Remove mushroom stems and chop. Cook bacon until crisp. Sautee mushroom stems, green pepper and onion, until tender. Pour off bacon fat. Add potatoes, crumbled bacon, chopped parsley, seasoned salt and pepper. Stuff mushroom caps. Place in shallow baking pan with small amount of water (water should be about ¼" deep). Bake in preheated oven (325°) for about 25 minutes. Makes 12 servings.

PICKLES

RELISH

JAMS

APPLE-CARROT RELISH

 6 carrots, pared and chopped fine
12 apples, peeled and chopped
 1 onion, chopped
 2 green peppers, seeded and chopped
 1 cup sugar
 2 cups cider vinegar
 1 lemon, sliced thin and seeded
1½ teaspoons each; salt and ground ginger
 1 cup seeded raisins

Combine all ingredients in a large saucepan and cook for 30 minutes, stirring occasionally, until mixture is thick. Spoon mixture into hot sterilized jars, seal, and cool. Makes about 2 quarts.

PINEAPPLE CARROT PICKLES

 4 medium carrots cut in ½-inch slices
 1 fresh pineapple
 3 cups brown sugar
 2 cups water
1½ cup vinegar
   dash salt
 2 sticks cinnamon
 1 tablespoon whole cloves

Peel pineapple. Cut fruit in 1-inch cubes. Combine sugar, water, vinegar and boil slowly for 15 minutes. Place spices in bag; add to syrup along with pineapple and carrots. Cover and simmer for 45 minutes. Remove pineapple and carrots and place in sterilized jars. Boil syrup for five minutes longer. Discard spices. Pour syrup over fruit and carrots and seal at once.

CARROT-CELERY RELISH

4 cups chopped carrots
4 cups chopped celery
2 sweet red peppers, seeded and chopped
2 green peppers, seeded and chopped
8 unpeeled apples, cored and chopped
3 cups sugar
1½ cups vinegar
1½ cups water
2 teaspoon mustard seed
2 teaspoon celery seed
1 teaspoon dill seed
2 tablespoons coarse pickling salt

Combine all the ingredients in a large pan. Bring to
a boil and simmer gently 25 to 30 minutes until the
carrots are tender. Pour into hot jars, leaving
half inch space from the top of the jar. Seal and
process in a boiling water bath for 20 minutes.
Remove the jars from the water bath and let cool.
Makes 5 pints.

CARROT JAM

12 medium carrots, chopped coarse
1 tablespoon salt
2 cups white vinegar
3 cups sugar

Add salt to carrots and let stand overnight. Drain
well, pressing out all liquid. Put in kettle with
sugar and vinegar. Cook, uncovered, for 45 minutes,
or until of marmalade consistency, stirring
frequently. Pour into hot sterilized jars and seal.
Makes four or five ½-pint jars.

PICKLED CARROTS

1 pound carrots
1½ cups white vinegar
½ cup water
1 cup sugar
3 tablespoons mixed pickling spice
1 cinnamon stick

Wash and pare carrots and cut into thin sticks.
Cook carrots in a little boiling salted water for
10 minutes, or until almost tender. Drain. Combine
remaining ingredients in a saucepan and simmer for
10 minutes; strain. Add carrot sticks; bring to
boil. After boiling for 2 minutes pack carrots into
hot sterilized jars. Pour syrup over carrots; seal.
Makes about 2 pints.

CARROT-ORANGE TOPPING

1 tablespoon grated orange peel
2 tablespoons grated lemon peel
4 cups water, divided
3 cups shredded, carrots (3 large)
1 cup orange juice
3 tablespoons lemon juice
3 cups sugar
  dash salt

In 3-quart saucepan cook orange and lemon peels
in 2 cups water 15 minutes. Add carrots and remaining
2 cups water. Cook 10 to 15 minutes or until
carrots are barely tender. Add orange and lemon
juices, sugar and salt. Boil until syrup reaches
220° on candy thermometer. Pour into hot sterilized
jars, leaving ¼-inch headspace. Seal jars and
process in simmering-water bath 10 minutes. Makes
4-½ cups. Delicious on pancakes, waffles,
and ice cream.

PENNSYLVANIA DUTCH CHOWCHOW

2 cups each of:
   sliced unpeeled cucumbers
   chopped sweet peppers
   chopped white cabbage
   sliced yellow onions
   chopped unpeeled green tomatoes
   lima beans
   cut green beans
   sliced carrots
   chopped celery
2 tablespoons celery seed
4 teaspoons mustard seed
4 cups cider vinegar
2 cups water
4 cups sugar
¼ cup ground turmeric

Soak cucumbers, peppers, cabbage, onions, and tomatoes in salted water overnight. Use ¼ cup salt for each quart of water. Cook lima beans, green beans, carrots, and celery until barely tender. Drain all vegetables well. Mix soaked and cooked vegetables with remaining ingredients. Bring to boil, lower heat, and simmer gently for 10 minutes. Place while hot in hot sterilized jars and seal at once. Makes 8 to 10 pints.

GOLDEN LEMON MARMALADE

1 pound carrots
2 medium lemons, quartered and seeded
4 cups sugar
½ teaspoon salt
½ cup water
½ cup sliced maraschino cherries

Chop carrots and lemon very finely. In large
kettle or Dutch oven, combine chopped carrot, chopped
lemon, sugar, salt and water Bring to full rolling
boil. Cook over medium high heat for 10 minutes.
Add sliced cherries; cook an additional 3 to 5
minutes or till thickened. Pour into clean, hot
jelly glasses; seal at once. Makes four ½-pints.

DILLED CARROT STICKS

2 pounds carrots
  salted water
1½ cups white vinegar
1½ cups water
½ teaspoon each of celery seed, caraway seed,
  and mustard seed
1 cup sugar
1 teaspoon coarse salt
½ teaspoon crushed hot peppers
1½ teaspoon dill seed

Wash and peel carrots and cut into thin sticks.
Cook in a little boiling salted water for about
10 minutes, or until almost tender. Drain; pack
carrots closely into hot sterilized pint jars.
Combine remaining ingredients in a saucepan. Bring
to a full rolling boil. After boiling for 2 minutes,
pour syrup over carrots to overflowing and seal
jars. Serve chilled with salads or sliced cold
meats. Makes 4 pints.

PICKLED BABY CARROTS

18 baby carrots, whole
 1 cup sugar
 1 cup vinegar
 1 cup water
 1 tablespoon mustard seed
2½ inches stick cinnamon, broken
 3 whole cloves

Precook carrots 5 minutes. Drain. Combine next
4 ingredients. Tie cinnamon and cloves in cloth
bag; add to sugar water mixture. Simmer 10 minutes;
pour over carrots. Cool; refrigerate 8 hours or
overnight.

TANGY RELISH MOLD

1 3-ounce package lemon-flavored gelatin
1 teaspoon salt
1 cup boiling water
¼ cup prepared horseradish
¼ cup prepared mustard
1 cup whipping cream, whipped
¼ cup sliced pimiento-stuffed green olives
¼ cup finely chopped celery
½ cup grated carrots

Dissolve gelatin and salt in boiling water. Divide
mixture in half. Stir horseradish into one half and
mustard into the other half. Beat each mixture until
smooth. Chill both until partially set. Fold half
the whipped cream and all the olives into the horseradish mixture. Fold remaining whipped cream, all
the celery and carrots into the mustard mixture.
Pour mustard mixture into 3 cup ring mold. Carefully
pour horseradish mixture over mustard mixture. Chill
until firm. Makes 12 servings.

HOT PICADILLY

3 cups sliced carrot rounds
1 small cauliflower, divided into flowerets
1 pound small white onions
1 yellow onion, cut into small pieces
1 cucumber, cut into small cubes
2 underripe tomatoes, cut into small pieces
2 cups green beans, cut into small pieces
1 cup coarse salt
2 quarts cold water
6 tablespoons flour
4 tablespoons dry mustard
2 teaspoons turmeric
1 quart vinegar
¼ cup sugar

Combine all the vegetables in a large bowl. Dissolve
the salt in water and add to the vegetables. Cover
and chill for 24 hours. Drain. To prepare the
sauce, combine the flour, mustard and turmeric. Add
½ cup vinegar and stir to form a smooth paste. Pour
the paste into a large saucepan and add the remaining
vinegar gradually. Heat to boiling. Add the sugar
and all of the vegetables. Simmer vegetables for
five minutes in the sauce. Spoon into hot sterilized
jars, seal and cool. Makes about 2 quarts.

CARROT-ONION RELISH

2 large carrots, chopped fine
1 large cucumber, seeded and chopped fine
1½ teaspoons salt
1 onion, minced
½ teaspoon pepper
1 cup white vinegar
½ pimiento, chopped

Combine cucumber and carrots with salt. Let drain
1 hour in colander. Add remaining ingredients.
Cover and store in refrigerator. Makes about 3 cups.

HAWAIIAN CHUTNEY

 2 large cans crushed pineapple or 1 large pineapple
1½ cups vinegar
1½ cups brown sugar
 2 tablespoons finely chopped fresh ginger or 3
   tablespoons candied ginger
 2 cups grated carrots
 5 cloves garlic, minced
 1 tablespoon salt
1½ cups raisins
 3 small red peppers or pickled red chili peppers,
   seeded and chopped
 1 cup chopped almonds

Combine pineapple, vinegar, brown sugar, ginger,
garlic and salt. Cook over low heat until pineapple
is tender-about 30 minutes. Add raisins, red
peppers and nuts and cook until chutney is thick.
Stir frequently. Pour into hot steralized jars and
seal immediately with parafin. Makes 2 quarts.

CARROT-ALMOND CONSERVE

 2 pounds carrots
 4 cups water
 2 lemons
 4 cups sugar
 ½ teaspoon salt
1½ cups slivered blanched almonds

Wash and trim carrots and force through food chopper.
Put in pot with water and cook, covered, for 10
minutes, or until almost tender. Do not drain.
Force lemons through food chopper and add to first
mixture. Add sugar and salt, cook rapidly for 25
minutes, or until thick, stirring occasionally.
Add almonds and pour into 8 hot sterilized ½-pint
jars. Seal at once. Makes 8 jars.

RAW CARROT RELISH

6 cups peeled and chopped carrots
3 cups chopped green peppers
3 cups chopped sweet red peppers
6 cups chopped cabbage
3 cups peeled and chopped onions
6 cups vinegar
2 cups sugar
3 tablespoons salt
1 tablespoon mustard seed
1 tablespoon celery seed
1 tablespoon whole allspice

Combine the vegetables thoroughly and pack into
sterilized jars. Mix the vinegar with the
remaining ingredients, bring to a boil and simmer
for five minutes. Pour the boiling vinegar over
the raw vegetables, making sure that they are
completely covered. Seal immediately and store
in the refrigerator. Makes 7 pints.

CALIFORNIA JAM

2 large oranges
6 cups diced rhubarb
3 cups ground raw carrots
3 cups light corn syrup
2 cups sugar

Remove seeds and grind oranges. Combine with
remaining ingredients and let stand overnight.
Bring to a boil and cook slowly until rhubarb
is transparent and mixture is thickened. Pour
into hot sterilized jars and seal. Makes ten
½-pint jars.

GRANDPA'S PICKLES

2 cups each of four vegetables: celery, carrots,
   green peppers, red peppers, cut into 1½" sticks
2 cups cauliflowerets
2 cups peeled pearl onions or sliced onions
4 cups white vinegar
1 cup sugar
1 teaspoon salt
1 tablespoon celery seed
2 teaspoons dry mustard
2 teaspoons turmeric
2 cloves garlic, minced
1 small bay leaf
2 dried hot red peppers

In a large saucepan, cook each variety of
vegetables, except onions, individually in boiling
water for 2 minutes. Remove and cool under cold
water. Drain. Layer vegetables in 2 quart jar.
In separate saucepan, combine vinegar, sugar, salt,
spices and hot peppers. Bring to a boil. Pour
over vegetables. Let cool. Cover and refrigerate
at least 10 days before serving.

CARROT RELISH

1½ cups chopped carrots
1 lemon
1 cup chopped onions
½ cup catsup
2 tablespoons chopped green pepper
1 tablespoon chopped red pepper
1 tablespoon tomato paste
4 teaspoons salad oil
2 teaspoons cider vinegar
½ teaspoon cayenne pepper
½ teaspoon turmeric
½ teaspoon crushed red pepper

Peel lemon and finely mince enough lemon peel to
equal 2 tablespoons. In a small bowl, mix lemon
peel and remaining ingredients. Cover and refrigerate
for up to 4 hours. Makes about 2¼ cups.

PANCAKES
WAFFLES
BREAD

NANA'S SCONES

1 package active dry yeast
1 cup water (reserved from cooking water from potatoes)
2 eggs
½ cup sugar
1 tablespoon salt
  cooking oil
1½ cups mashed potatoes
½ cup nonfat dry-milk solids
4½ to 5 cups sifted all-purpose flour

Sprinkle or crumble yeast into water. Use very
warm water (105° to 115° F.) for dry yeast, let stand
for 10 minutes; then stir until dissolved. In large
bowl put eggs, sugar, salt, 1/3 cup oil, potatoes,
milk and yeast mixture. Beat at low speed until
well blended. Gradually add 2 cups flour and beat
well. Add remaining 2½ to 3 cups flour by hand.
Mix until the dough forms a ball away from the sides
of the bowl. Let rise until double in size. Roll
out on a floured board until about ½-inch thick.
Cut into 3" squares. Fry in 1-inch hot oil turning
when golden brown. Makes about 30 scones.

CREAM CARROT BISCUITS

2 cups biscuit mix
1 cup sour cream
¼ cup grated carrots
1 tablespoon snipped chives

Heat oven to 450°. Mix all ingredients until soft
dough forms; beat vigorously 20 strokes. Gently
smooth dough into ball on floured cloth-covered
board. Knead 5 times. Roll dough ½ inch thick.
Cut with floured 2" cutter. Place on ungreased
cookie sheet. Bake until golden brown, 8 to 10
minutes. Makes 10 to 12 biscuits.

GLAZED POTATO DOUGHNUTS

1 cup milk
¼ cup granulated sugar
1 teaspoon salt
¼ cup butter or regular margarine
1 package active dry yeast
¼ cup warm water
1 cup unseasoned mashed potato
2 eggs
5½ cups sifted all-purpose flour
    Salad oil or shortening for frying

Glaze

3 cups confectioners sugar
1 teaspoon vanilla extract

In small saucepan, heat milk until bubbles form
around edge of pan; remove from heat. Add
granulated sugar, salt and butter; stir until
butter is melted. Let cool to lukewarm. In
large bowl, sprinkle yeast over warm water. Stir
until dissolved. Add the lukewarm milk mixture,
mashed potato, eggs and 2 cups flour. Beat until
smooth. Add remaining flour and beat until smooth.
Cover with towel; let rise in warm place until
double in size-about 1 hour. Punch down dough.
Turn out onto well-floured surface; turn over to
coat with flour. Knead ten times or until the
dough is smooth. Cover with bowl and let set
for 10 minutes. Roll out dough ½-inch thick. Cut
with floured 3-inch doughnut cutter. Let rise 45 minute
or until doubled. Heat 1-1½ inches oil or shortening
in electric skillet or heavy saucepan to 375°. Gently
drop doughnuts into hot oil. As they rise to the
surface turn over. Fry until brown on both sides-
about 3 minutes total. Drain well on paper towels.
Make glaze; in small bowl combine confectioners
sugar, vanilla and 6 tablespoons water; use to glaze
warm doughnuts. Makes 20.

MEXICAN-POTATO CAKES

2½ cups mashed potatoes
 ½ cup yellow corn meal
 ½ cup grated sharp Cheddar cheese
 ¼ teaspoon marjoram
 ¼ teaspoon thyme
 ¼ cup milk
     butter or oil for frying

Mix all ingredients and knead to smooth dough.
Divide into 8 portions. Shape into 3-inch
round cakes. Fry in hot buttered skillet turning
once until crisp and golden on both sides. Makes
8 cakes.

CARROT CLOVERLEAF ROLLS

1 package active dry yeast
4 to 4½ cups sifted all-purpose flour
1 cup milk
4 medium carrots, cooked and mashed (1 cup)
½ cup brown sugar
6 tablespoons butter
½ teaspoon salt

In large bowl, combine yeast and 1½ cups of the
flour. Heat together milk, carrot, brown sugar,
butter and salt until warm, stirring to melt
butter. Add to dry ingredients in bowl; beat at
low speed for ½ minute. Beat 3 minutes at high
speed. By hand, stir in enough of the remaining
flour to make a stiff dough. Turn out on a lightly
floured surface and knead well. Place in greased
bowl; turn once. Cover and let rise until double,
about 1 hour. Punch down; let rest 10 minutes.
Divide dough into 18 equal parts. Shape each part
into three 1-inch balls. For each roll, place
3 balls in greased muffin pan. Let rise again
until almost double, 30 to 45 minutes. Bake at
400° for 15 to 20 minutes. Brush tops with a
little melted butter while hot. Makes 18 rolls.

SALT-RISING BREAD

3 medium potatoes, pared and cut up
½ cup all-purpose flour
2 tablespoons sugar
2 packages active dry yeast
½ cup sugar
¼ cup cooking oil
2 teaspoons salt
8 to 8¼ cups all-purpose flour

Cook potatoes, covered, in 6 cups unsalted water until tender; drain, reserving 5 cups cooking water. Cool. (Use potatoes for another purpose.) To make starter, combine the ½ cup flour, 2 tablespoons sugar, 1 cup potato water, and yeast. Cover; let stand in warm place several hours. Add remaining 4 cups potato water and ½ cup sugar. Cover; let stand in warm place overnight. Next day, stir starter; remove 1 cup. Add 2 tablespoons sugar to starter; pour into pint jar. Cover; store in refrigerator until ready to use. To the remaining starter (4 cups) add oil, salt and enough flour to make a moderately stiff dough. Place in large greased bowl. Let rise in warm place until double, about 1 hour. Stir down. Place in greased 12x5½-inch dishpan. Let rise until nearly double, about 1 hour. Bake at 350º for 60 to 70 minutes. To use reserved starter, proceed as before except substiture the 1 cup reserved starter for the 1 cup potato water.

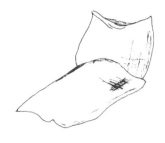

MASHED-POTATO SCONES

3 cups biscuit mix
¼ cup sugar
2 eggs
1 cup mashed potato
2 tablespoons butter or margarine, melted
1 egg white, slightly beaten

In large mixing bowl, combine biscuit mix, sugar,
eggs and mashed potato; mix until smooth. Turn
out dough onto lightly floured surface. Knead 5
times. Roll dough to ¼-inch thick. Cut into 2½
inch squares. Brush with melted butter; fold over
to make a triangle, pressing edges lightly to seal.
Place on lightly greased baking sheet 2-inches apart.
Brush with egg white. Bake at 400° for 8 to 10
minutes, or until golden-brown. Makes 1½ dozen.

HONEY-WHEAT MUFFINS

1 egg
1 cup milk
¼ cup oil
¼ cup honey
1 cup grated carrots
1 cup whole-wheat flour
1 cup white flour
3 teaspoons baking powder
1 teaspoon salt

Grease bottoms of 12 muffin cups with margarine
or shortening. Beat egg, milk and oil with a fork
in medium bowl until well blended. Add honey and
mix. In another bowl, mix dry ingredients. Mix
thoroughly. Add dry mixture to egg mixture and
stir until moist and lumpy. Spoon batter into
muffin cups 2/3 full. Bake at 400° for 20 to
25 minutes. Cool slightly, remove from muffin
pan.

27

POTATO WAFFLES

3 eggs
1 cup sifted all-purpose flour
2 teaspoons baking powder
½ teaspoon salt
1 cup milk
1 tablespoon melted shortening
2 cups cold mashed potatoes
  butter
  maple syrup

Beat eggs until light. Add sifted dry ingredients, milk, and shortening; mix until smooth. Add potatoes and mix well. Bake in hot waffle iron. Serve hot with butter and syrup. Makes 4 servings.

CARROT BREAD

4 eggs
2 cups sugar
1¼ cups salad oil
3 cups all-purpose flour, unsifted
2 teaspoons baking powder
1½ teaspoons soda
¼ teaspoon salt
2 teaspoons ground cinnamon
2 cups finely shredded raw carrots
1 tablespoon vanilla
½ to 1 cup raisins

Beat eggs; gradually add sugar, beating until thick. Gradually add oil and continue beating until thoroughly blended. In separate bowl, stir together flour, baking powder, soda, salt and cinnamon until blended. Mix dry ingredients into egg mixture until smooth. Stir in carrots, vanilla and raisins. Spoon into 2 well greased 9x5-inch loaf pans. Bake at 350° for 1 hour, or until toothpick inserted in middle comes out clean.

SOUTHERN PANCAKES

1½ cups sifted all-purpose flour
3½ teaspoons baking powder
 1 teaspoon salt
 ½ teaspoon ground nutmeg
1¼ cups mashed cooked sweet potatoes
 2 eggs, beaten
1½ cups milk
 ¼ cup butter, melted

Sift dry ingredients into bowl. Combine remaining
ingredients and add to flour. Mix only until blended.
Drop by tablespoonfuls onto hot greased griddle and
fry until browned. Makes 24 pancakes.

SWEET-POTATO WAFFLES

 2 cups sifted all-purpose flour
 3 teaspoons baking powder
 1 teaspoon salt
 ¼ teaspoon ground cinnamon
 3 eggs separated
1½ cups milk
 1 cup mashed cooked sweet potatoes
 ¼ cup butter or margarine, melted
 ½ cup chopped nuts
   maple syrup

Sift together flour, baking powder, salt, and
cinnamon. Beat egg whites until stiff. Beat egg
yolks; add milk and potatoes. Beat until blended.
Add to dry ingredients with butter and mix well. Fold
in egg whites and nuts. Bake. Serve hot with syrup.
Makes 4 to 6 servings.

SWEET-POTATO DOUGHNUTS

2 eggs, beaten
1 cup sugar
3 tablespoons shortening
1 cup mashed cooked sweet potatoes
¼ cup milk
3½ cups sifted all-purpose flour
4 teaspoons baking powder
½ teaspoon salt
¼ teaspoon each of ground nutmeg and cinnamon
    fat for deep frying

Combine first four ingredients and beat until well
blended. Add milk and sifted dry ingredients; mix well
Chill for 1 hour, or until firm enough to roll. Roll
on lightly flour board to ½-inch thickness and cut
with floured 3-inch cutter. Fry in deep hot fat
until golden-brown and done. Drain. Makes 30.

POTATO CAKES

2 cups mashed potatoes
½ cup unsifted all-purpose flour
1 tablespoon butter
¼ teaspoon salt
¼ teaspoon double-acting baking powder
  Milk
2 tablespoons salad oil

Place potatoes in bowl. Add all ingredients
except milk and oil. Mix to a smooth dough,
adding a little milk if necessary. Turn onto
floured surface, knead until smooth. Divide
dough in half. Roll each half into a circle
¼-inch thick. Cut each circle into 8 wedges.
Heat oil in skillet. Cook wedges over medium-
high heat until browned on both sides, about 3
minutes. Drain on paper towels. Makes 16.

BOSTON CARROT BREAD

1 package Gingerbread Mix
1 cup yellow corn meal
1 cup all-purpose flour
1 cup seedless raisins
1¼ cups water
1 cup grated carrots

Combine all ingredients in large mixing bowl. Mix
with spoon until all dry ingredients are moistened.
Pour batter into greased 9x5-inch pan. Bake at
375° for 35 to 40 minutes. Remove from pan
immediately. Makes 1 loaf.

POTATO ROLLS

1 package active dry yeast
¼ cup warm water
½ cup hot mashed potatoes
¼ cup shortening
¼ cup sugar
1½ teaspoons salt
1 cup milk, scalded
1 egg
4 to 4½ cups sifted all-purpose flour

Soften yeast in warm water. Combine potatoes,
shortening, sugar, salt, and hot milk. Cool to
lukewarm. Add softened yeast and egg. Stir in
2 cups of flour; beat well. Stir in remaining
flour. Knead on lightly floured surface until
smooth and elastic. Place in lightly greased
bowl, turning once to grease surface. Cover;
let rise until double (about 1 hour). Punch down.
Shape in ball. Cover and let rest 10 minutes.
Shape in rolls; place on greased baking sheet. Let
rise until almost double (about 1 hour). Bake
at 400° 10 to 12 minutes. Makes 2 dozen.

SWEET-POTATO BISCUITS

1½ cups flour
2 tablespoons sugar
3 teaspoons baking powder
1 teaspoon salt
   dash of nutmeg
1 cup mashed cooked sweet potato
2/3 cup milk
6 tablespoons oil

In large bowl mix flour, sugar, baking powder, salt
and nutmeg; set aside. In small bowl mix sweet
potato, milk and oil; stir into flour mixture just
to moisten. Turn out on floured surface. Knead
gently about 6 strokes. Pat out about ½-inch
thick. Cut with floured 1-3/4 inch cutter. Bake
on ungreased cookie sheet at 450° for 12 minutes
or until puffed and lightly browned. Makes about
12 biscuits.

CRUNCHY MUNCHY MUFFINS

2 cups flour
1 tablespoon sugar
1 tablespoon baking powder
½ teaspoon salt
1 can (10½ ounce) condensed cream of celery soup
1 egg, beaten
¼ cup cooking oil
3½ ounce can French fried onions, crumbled
½ cup crushed potato chips
½ cup grated Cheddar cheese

In large bowl, combine flour, sugar, baking powder and
salt. Combine undiluted soup, egg and oil. Add all
at once to dry ingredients; stir just until all dry
particles are moistened. Stir in onions. Fill greased
muffin cups 2/3 full. Combine potato chips and cheese;
sprinkle over muffins. Bake at 400° for 18 to 20
minutes or until golden brown. Makes 12 to 15 muffins.

CARROT BRAN MUFFINS

2 cups whole wheat flour
1 cup bran
½ cup wheat germ
½ teaspoon salt
1 teaspoon baking powder
1 teaspoon soda
1 cup shredded carrot
1 cup seedless raisins
1 cup chopped nuts
1 egg, slightly beaten
1¼ cups buttermilk
½ cup vegetable oil
6 tablespoons melted butter

Preheat oven to 400º. Prepare muffin cups by
greasing well or lining with paper cups. Combine
dry ingredients in mixing bowl, mix well. Add
carrots, raisins and nuts. Add remaining ingredients
and stir just enough to moisten. Spoon into muffin
cups, filling 3/4 full. Bake 15 to 20 minutes.
Makes 18 to 20 muffins.

PAM'S POTATO PANCAKES

1 cup finely grated raw potato
1 teaspoon minced onions
2 eggs
1 cup sifted flour
2 teaspoons baking powder
½ teaspoon salt
  pinch pepper
2 teaspoons sugar
1 cup milk
2 tablespoons melted shortening

Add liquid to dry ingredients, mix well until
blended. Bake on hot griddle turning once only.

POTATO PANCAKES

4 large potatoes, peeled
1 small onion
½ cup milk
¼ cup flour
1 egg, beaten
1 teaspoon salt
  shortening
  applesauce

Grate potatoes and onion into milk; blend in flour,
egg and salt. In large skillet heat 1 inch shortening
until hot; drop rounded tablespoonfuls of batter
into shortening and brown on both sides. Drain
on paper towels. Serve at once with warm applesauce.
Makes about 3 dozen.

WHEAT GERM LOAF

1½ cups minced celery
 1 cup grated carrots
 ½ cup minced onion
 ¼ cup minced green pepper
 ½ cup butter
 2 cups cooked rice
1½ cups chopped pecans
 1 cup wheat germ
 2 tablespoons chopped pimiento
 1 teaspoon salt
   dash pepper
 4 eggs, beaten

Saute celery, carrots, onion and green pepper in
butter until onion is soft but not brown. Combine
with rice, pecans, wheat germ, pimiento, salt,
pepper and eggs. Mix well. Pack into greased 9x5x3
inch loaf pan. Bake at 375° 40 to 50 minutes. Let
stand in pan 5 minutes before removing. Makes
6 to 8 servings.

SOUPS

CASSOULET CHOWDER

1¼ cups dry pinto beans
4 cups water
1 (12 ounce) package cooked sausage links
2 cups cubed cooked chicken
2 cups cubed cooked ham
2 to 3 medium carrots, peeled and sliced
1 (8 ounce) can tomato sauce
1 cup dry red wine
½ cup chopped onion
½ teaspoon garlic powder
1 bay leaf

In a large saucepan combine beans and water; bring
to boil. Reduce heat; cover and simmer 1½ hours.
Refrigerate beans and liquid several hours or
overnight. In a 3½-4 quart pan combine beans
and liquid, and remaining ingredients. Cover and
cook on low for 4 hours. Season to taste with
salt and pepper. Makes 8 to 10 servings.

SALMON POTATO SOUP

2 slices of bacon, diced
1 onion, minced
3 cups diced potatoes
3 cups water
1 cup grated raw carrot
2 teaspoons salt
¼ teaspoon pepper
2 tablespoons all-purpose flour
3 cups milk
1 can (1 pound) salmon

Cook bacon in kettle until golden brown. Remove
bacon. Add onion to fat remaining in kettle and
cook until golden. Add potatoes and water, cover
and simmer for 15 minutes, or until tender. Add
carrot and seasonings. Blend flour with a little
of the milk. Stir into hot mixture and cook,
stirring, until slightly thickened. Add salmon,
remaining milk and heat. Sprinkle with bacon. Makes
4 servings.

CARROT VICHYSSOISE

2 cups potatoes, diced
1¼ cups carrots, sliced
1 leek, sliced
3 cups chicken broth
1 cup cream
1 teaspoon salt
   pinch white pepper
   shredded carrot and parsley, for garnish

In large saucepan combine potatoes, carrots, leek and chicken broth; bring to a boil and simmer 25 minutes. Pour half the soup into blender and blend until smooth. Pour into large bowl. Repeat with remaining soup. Add cream, salt and pepper. Cover and refrigerate until well chilled. Serve in chilled bowls; garnish with carrot and parsley. Makes 6 to 8 servings.

GAZPACHO

6 cups tomato juice
1 tablespoon sugar
1½ teaspoons salt
1 clove garlic, crushed
3 tablespoons lemon juice
¼ cup olive oil
1 teaspoon Worcestershire sauce
1 cucumber, pared, seeded, and shredded
1 large green pepper, halved, shredded
1 cup shredded carrots
1 cup chopped celery
¼ cup chopped green onion
2 large tomatoes, chopped
   Garlic Croutons

Combine tomato juice, sugar, salt, garlic, lemon juice, oil and Worcestershire in large bowl. Beat with rotary mixer to blend. Stir in cucumber, green pepper, carrots, celery, onion and tomatoes. Cover and chill overnight. Serve with Garlic Croutons.

LENTIL-TURNIP SOUP WITH DUMPLINGS

2 medium white turnips, sliced thin
1 cup thinly sliced carrots
1 cup chopped green pepper
1 medium onion, sliced
1 clove garlic, crushed
3 tablespoons butter
1 cup dried lentils
4 cups water
2 beef bouillon cubes
1 teaspoon salt
1 bay leaf, crumbled
1½ cups milk
  dumplings

In 4-quart pot or dutch oven over low heat saute
turnips, carrots, green pepper, onion and garlic
in butter about 10 minutes or until crisp-tender
but not browned. Add lentils, water, bouillon
cubes, salt and bay leaf. Bring to boil; reduce
heat; cover and, simmer about 40 minutes, stirring
occasionally. Stir in milk. Continue cooking
on low heat until soup is hot (do not boil). Drop
dumplings into hot soup. Cover and simmer 15 minutes
or until dumplings are cooked. Makes 4 servings.

DUMPLINGS

6 tablespoons butter, softened
1 cup shredded Cheddar cheese
½ cup flour
¼ cup diced bologna
¼ cup minced onion
1 egg
½ teaspoon each-dry mustard and oregano

Mix all ingredients well, in small bowl. With
floured hands shape in twenty 1-inch balls.

LAND'S END CHOWDER

3 slices bacon, cut into ½-inch pieces
1 medium onion, sliced
2 medium potatoes, cubed
2½ cups hot water
1½ teaspoons salt
¼ teaspoon pepper
1 package frozen cod fillets, 16 ounces
1 can (16 ounce) whole kernal corn, drained
1 can (5.3 ounces) evaporated milk
2 tablespoons butter

In large saucepan cook bacon until crispy. Add
onion and saute until tender. Add potatoes, water,
salt and pepper. Bring to boil over medium heat.
Cover; reduce heat and simmer until potatoes are tender
but still firm. Add frozen fish; cook, covered, 8 to
10 minutes, stirring until fish breaks up easily.
Stir in corn and milk. Cook, covered, until heated
thoroughly. Add butter and serve immediately. Makes
4 to 6 servings.

CURRY POTATO SOUP

3 cups diced raw potatoes
2½ cups boiling water
3 chicken or beef bouillon cubes
1 teaspoon salt
1 garlic clove, minced
1½ teaspoons curry powder
1 small onion, chopped
2 cups milk
2 tablespoons butter or margarine
¼ teaspoon pepper

Combine potatoes, water bouillon cubes, salt, garlic,
curry powder, and onion. Cover and cook until
potatoes fall apart, 40 to 50 minutes. Remove from
heat and mash potatoes in the liquid. Add milk,
butter, and pepper. Heat only until hot. Makes
6 servings.

SWISS CAULIFLOWER SOUP

2 cans (10-3/4 ounce) condensed chicken broth
3 medium leeks, washed and thinly sliced
3 medium carrots, pared and thinly sliced
2 medium onions, peeled
4 whole cloves
1 teaspoon dried marjoram leaves
½ teaspoon ground celery seed
¼ teaspoon white pepper
½ teaspoon nutmeg
1 teaspoon salt
1 head cauliflower
½ cup heavy cream
2 egg yolks
1 tablespoon cornstarch
8 ounces Swiss cheese, cut in 4x2¼-inch strips

In 8-quart pan combine chicken broth and 4 cups water; mix well. Add leeks, carrots, 1 onion cut in quarters and 1 onion studded with the cloves. Add marjoram, celery seed, pepper, nutmeg and salt. Bring to boil; reduce heat and simmer, covered, 15 minutes. Meanwhile, wash cauliflower; separate into large flowerets; add to soup. Bring back to boiling; reduce heat and simmer, uncovered, 30 minutes. In small bowl, combine cream, egg yolks and cornstarch; mix until smooth. Stir in a little of the hot soup; mix well. Stir into rest of hot soup. Bring to boil. Serve in casserole with cheese arranged in lattice fashion on top. Put under broiler just to melt cheese. Makes 6 to 8 servings.

ANDES SHRIMP AND CORN MAIN-DISH CHOWDER

¼ cup chopped green onions
1 small clove garlic, minced
   dash cayenne pepper
1 tablespoon butter
2 cans Cream of Potato Soup
1 package (3 ounces) cream cheese, softened
1½ soup cans milk
2 cups small shrimp
1 can (8 ounces) whole kernel corn, undrained

In saucepan, cook onions with garlic and pepper
in butter until tender. Blend in soup, cream
cheese, and milk; add shrimp and corn. Bring to
boil; reduce heat. Cover; simmer. Makes 4 to 6
servings.

HAMBURGER-VEGETABLE SOUP

1½ pounds ground beef
 3 cups water
 3 medium carrots, chopped
 2 medium stalks celery, chopped
 1 large potato, pared and cut into ½-inch pieces
 2 medium onions, chopped
 2 teaspoons salt
 ¼ to ½ teaspoon pepper
 1 teaspoon bottled gravy coloring
 1 bay leaf
   dash leaf basil, crumbled
 1 can (28 ounces) tomatoes

Cook ground beef in Dutch oven, stirring constantly,
until light brown; drain. Stir in water, carrots,
celery, potato, onions, salt, pepper, gravy coloring
bay leaf and basil. Add tomatoes, breaking up with
a spoon. Heat to boil; lower heat; cover. Simmer
about 20 minutes or just until vegetables are
tender. Add additional salt and pepper if needed.
Makes 6 servings.

CLAM CHOWDER

4 slices bacon, minced
1 onion, chopped
2 6½ ounce cans minced clams
1 10½ ounce can condensed beef broth
1 soup can water
1 1 pound can stewed tomatoes
1 medium potato, peeled, diced
3 carrots, diced
1 bay leaf
1 teaspoon marjoram
½ teaspoon salt
   dash each-thyme and pepper
½ cup dry sherry

In a 3-quart pot, cook bacon until brown. Remove
from pan; drain and set aside. Add onion to
drippings and saute until golden, about 7 minutes.
Strain liquid from clams, adding juice to pot and
setting aside clams until later. Stir in broth,
water, tomatoes, potatoes, carrots and seasonings.
Simmer uncovered 20 minutes until vegetables are tender.
Discard bay leaf. Add bacon, clams and sherry.
Simmer 10 minutes. Serves 4.

CHEESY CHICKEN VEGETABLE MAIN-DISH SOUP

1 cup sliced zucchini
2 cups sliced carrots
1 small onion, sliced
1 tablespoon oregano leaves, crushed
2 tablespoon butter
1 can Cheddar Cheese Soup
1 can Cream of Potato Soup
1 soup can water
1 cup tomato juice
1½ cups cubed cooked chicken or turkey
½ teaspoon hot sauce

In large covered pan, cook zucchini, carrot, onion with
oregano in butter until tender. Add remaining ingredients. Heat well. Makes 4 to 6 servings.

14-CARROT COLD

3 tablespoons butter
1½ cups onion, finely chopped
1 celery stalk with leaves, finely chopped
14 baby carrots, cut in ¼-inch rounds
2 medium potatoes, peeled and diced
1 teaspoon sugar
1 tablespoon chopped fresh dill
3 cups chicken broth
1 cup milk
1 cup heavy cream
   pinch cayenne pepper
   salt and pepper to taste
   Garnish: chopped fresh parsley

Melt butter in 3-quart saucepan. Add onion and celery and saute until onion is translucent. Add carrots, potatoes, sugar, dill and broth. Cook, covered, on low heat 25 minutes. Cool slightly and puree in blender. Replace in saucepan. Cover and chill. Just before serving, add milk, cream, cayenne, salt and pepper. Garnish. Serves 8.

SEAFOOD MUSHROOM CHOWDER

¼ cup diced onion
¼ cup diced green pepper
2 tablespoons oil
1 (10½ ounce) can chicken broth
1¼ cups water
1 cup fresh mushrooms
1 teaspoon salt
   dash thyme
1 pound haddock fillets, cubed
1 (10 ounce) package frozen peas and carrots
1 cup potatoes, cubed
1 cup cooked shrimp
2 tablespoons cornstarch
½ cup half and half

   (CONTINUED)

42

Cook mushrooms, onion and green pepper in oil. Add
chicken broth, water, salt, thyme, fish, peas and
carrots and potatoes. Bring to boil. Cover and
simmer 10 minutes. Add shrimp. Combine cornstarch
and half and half and stir into chowder. Heat
over low heat until thickened. Makes 8 servings.

POLISH BORSCHT

2 quarts beef bouillon
1 large onion, chopped
3 large dried mushrooms, washed, soaked and chopped
3 cups shredded beets
1 cup shredded carrots
1 medium head cabbage, shredded
1 tablespoon chopped parsley
2 teaspoons sugar
2 teaspoons lemon juice
1 cup dairy sour cream
6 small, hot potatoes, cooked and peeled

Simmer bouillon and onion together for about 2
hours. Strain and remove fat from stock. Add
mushrooms to stock and simmer for 20 minutes. Toss
beets, carrots, cabbage and parsley with sugar and
let mixture stand for 15 minutes. Add with lemon
juice to stock. Bring to gentle boil and boil for
25 to 30 minutes or until vegetables are tender.
Remove from heat, strain out vegetables. Stir
sour cream into stock and reheat but do not allow
to boil. Serve in soup plate with a potato in
center of each. Makes 6 servings.

CREAMY TUNA-POTATO SOUP

1 tablespoon margarine
4 green onions, sliced thin
2½ cups frozen hashed brown potatoes
3 cups chicken broth
1 can (13 ounces) evaporated milk
2 cans (about 7 ounces each) tuna
1 teaspoon dillweed
½ teaspoon pepper

In large saucepan melt margarine. Add green
onions and saute until tender. Add potatoes and
broth; cook over medium heat about 5 minutes or
until potatoes are tender. Stir in remaining
ingredients. Heat thoroughly. Makes 4 servings.

CHEESE AND BEER SOUP

¼ cup butter
¼ cup grated celery
¼ cup grated carrot
¼ cup finely chopped green pepper
¼ cup finely chopped onion
¼ cup all-purpose flour
3 (13-3/4 ounce) cans chicken broth
1 teaspoon salt
¼ teaspoon white pepper
3 cups grated sharp Cheddar cheese
1 (12 ounce) bottle or can light beer, room temp.

In large saucepan melt butter or margarine. Add
celery, carrot, green pepper and onion. Cook over
low heat until soft. Add flour. Blend in chicken
broth, salt and pepper. Cook, stirring constantly
until mixture thickens. Strain soup to remove
vegetables. Place vegetables in blender. Puree.
Return to saucepan. Place soup over low heat.
Add cheese ½ cup at a time, stirring until melted.
Blend in beer. Heat thoroughly. Do not boil.
Serves 6 to 8.

SWEET POTATO SOUP

3 medium sweet potatoes, peeled
2 quarts water
½ cup butter, clarified
1 large onion, finely chopped
2 stalks, celery, finely chopped
1 garlic clove, minced
¼ cup all-purpose flour
1 quart chicken broth
1 cup pineapple juice
 dash white pepper
½ cup instant potatoes
 salt to taste

Boil sweet potatoes in water in large saucepan until
soft, about 45 minutes. Remove potatoes and set
aside to cool. Reserve 2 cups of the cooking
liquid. Meanwhile heat butter in medium skillet.
Add onion, celery and garlic and saute until tender.
Remove and set aside. In skillet stir in flour
and blend until smooth. Remove from heat and set
aside. Mash sweet potatoes. Combine with reserved
cooking liquid, onion mixture, chicken broth,
pineapple juice and white pepper in another large
saucepan. Bring to boil, stirring several times.
Blend 2 tablespoons hot soup into butter/flour
mixture, then add to soup, stirring constantly.
Cover and simmer 20 minutes. Stir in instant
potatoes and simmer 10 more minutes. Add more
chicken broth if thinner consistency is desired
and season with salt to taste.

MUSHROOM AND LEEK BISQUE

1 pound mushrooms, sliced
1 bunch leeks, white part only, sliced
½ cup butter
1½ cups carrots, grated
4 tablespoons flour
1 teaspoon salt
¼ teaspoon white pepper
3 cans (13-3/4 ounces each) chicken broth
1 cup light cream

Saute mushrooms, leeks and carrots in butter in large saucepan until tender. Stir in flour, salt, pepper and 2 cans of chicken broth. Cook, stirring constantly, until mixture comes to a boil. Reduce heat; cover; simmer 20 minutes. Remove from heat; cool slightly. Pour mixture, a little at a time, into blender; puree. Pour into large bowl. When all the soup is pureed, pour back into large saucepan. Add remaining can of chicken broth and the light cream; heat until thoroughly hot. Garnish with whipped cream and chopped parsley if desired.

RUTABAGA-POTATO SOUP

1 small rutabaga
1 teaspoon salt
3 medium potatoes, peeled and thinly sliced
2 cups milk
1 teaspoon sugar
1 cup chicken broth or bouillon
2 tablespoons butter
   salt and pepper to taste

Peel rutabaga and cut in small pieces. Add salt and 1½ cups water. Cook, covered, 15 to 20 minutes. Add potatoes and cook about 10 minutes (do not drain). Mash, add milk and remaining ingredients and heat. Makes about 1½ quarts, or 6 servings.

SALADS

CURRIED CARROT AND ZUCCHINI SALAD

3 medium zucchini
3 carrots
3 green onions
2 tablespoons lemon juice
½ cup olive oil
1 teaspoon curry powder
1 teaspoon salt
¼ teaspoon pepper

Slice zucchini and carrots very thin into a
medium size bowl. Chop green onions, including
about 3 inches of the green tops and add to bowl.
Beat lemon juice, oil, curry, salt and pepper in
a cup; pour over vegetables. Toss to mix. Taste;
add additional salt and pepper if needed. Chill
several hours. Makes 6 servings.

HOT CARROT SALAD

6 medium-size carrots
1 teaspoon butter
4 large lettuce leaves
½ teaspoon salt
½ teaspoon crumbled dried thyme
½ teaspoon celery seed
3 tablespoons dairy sour cream
  salt and pepper to taste

Wash and scrape carrots. Slice diagonally. Use
butter to grease a small skillet. Line skillet with
2 lettuce leaves. Add carrots and salt. Top with
remaining lettuce leaves. Cover pan and cook until
the carrots are tender. Remove lettuce and add
thyme and celery seed. Stir in sour cream and salt
and pepper to taste. Reheat slightly and serve hot.
Makes 4 to 6 servings.

SOUR-CREAM POTATO SALAD

1 quart peeled and diced cooked potatoes
1 medium onion, chopped fine
½ cup diced celery
½ cup green pepper, diced
½ cup diced cucumber
½ cup thinly sliced radishes
1 tablespoon chopped chives
4 hard-cooked eggs
1 cup sour cream
¼ cup mayonnaise
½ teaspoon salt
  dash pepper
  dash each; garlic salt and cayenne
2 tablespoons vinegar
½ teaspoon hot prepared mustard

Combine potatoes, onion, celery, cucumber, radishes
and chives. Dice whites of 3 eggs and add to
vegetables. In bowl mash 3 egg yolks with fork; stir
in sour cream, mayonnaise, salt, pepper, garlic salt,
cayenne, vinegar and mustard. Add to vegetables and
mix well. Garnish with remaining egg, sliced. Chill
several hours. Makes 6 to 8 servings.

POTATOES IN THEIR JACKETS SALAD

12 small new red-skinned potatoes, unpeeled and halved
 ¼ cup cider vinegar
 ½ cup salad oil
 2 teaspoons seasoned salt
 2 tablespoons chopped parsley
 2 strips bacon, cooked & crumbled

Cook potatoes in a small amount of water in covered
pan just until tender; drain. Do not over cook.
Chill in refrigerator. Combine vinegar, oil, salt,
and parsley. Mix well and pour over potatoes, tossing
gently to coat well. Sprinkle with crumbled bacon.
Makes 6 servings.

DUBLIN POTATO SALAD

1 teaspoon each celery seed and mustard seed
2 tablespoons vinegar
3 cups warm diced cooked potatoes
2 teaspoons sugar
½ teaspoon salt
1 (12-ounce) can corned beef, chilled and diced
2 cups finely shredded crisp cabbage
¼ cup finely chopped dill pickle
¼ cup chopped green onions
1 cup mayonnaise or salad dressing
2 tablespoons milk
1 tablespoon vinegar
½ teaspoon salt

Soak celery and mustard seeds in 2 tablespoons vinegar; drizzle over warm potatoes. Sprinkle with sugar and ½ teaspoon salt. Chill. Add meat, cabbage, pickle, and onions. Mix remaining ingredients; pour over potato mixture; toss lightly. Makes 7 or 8 servings.

HARVEST RING

2 packages (3 ounce) lemon flavor gelatin
½ teaspoon salt
2 cups boiling water
1½ cups cold water
1 tablespoon vinegar
½ cup shredded carrots
½ cup chopped green pepper
½ cup chopped celery
1 tablespoon grated onion

Dissolve gelatin and salt in boiling water. Add cold water and vinegar; chill until thickened. Fold in vegetables and pour into 4-cup mold. Chill until firm, about 3 hours. Unmold. Garnish with crisp salad greens.

HERBED CARROT POTATO SALAD

1 cup mayonnaise or salad dressing
1 cup dairy sour cream
3 tablespoons lemon juice
2 tablespoons snipped chives
1 tablespoon worcestershire sauce
1 teaspoon salt
½ teaspoon dried dillweed
½ teaspoon dry mustard
   dash pepper
4 medium carrots, thinly bias-sliced
8 medium potatoes, cooked, peeled, and sliced
1 cup thinly bias-sliced celery
½ cup pitted ripe olives, sliced
   leaf lettuce
   carrot curls
   pitted ripe olives

Combine mayonnaise or salad dressing, sour cream,
lemon juice, chives, worcestershire, salt, dillweed,
mustard, and pepper until well combined. In a
medium saucepan heat a small amount of water to
boiling; add carrots and simmer, uncovered, for 2
minutes. Drain. Add to potatoes, celery, olives
and dressing mixture. Toss until well coated.
Let stand in refrigerator for several hours or
overnight. Garnish with olives and carrot curls
before servings. Makes 12 servings.

CARROT-COCONUT SALAD

 1 cup flaked coconut
1½ cups shredded raw carrots
 ¼ cup seedless raisins
 2 tablespoons fresh lemon juice
 1 cup mandarin oranges, drained
 ½ cup mayonnaise
   salt to taste
   salad greens

Mix all ingredients except greens. Chill and serve
on greens. Makes 4 to 6 servings.

CHEESY COLESLAW MOLD

    1 3-ounce package lime-flavored gelatin
    1½ cups boiling water
    2 tablespoons vinegar
    ½ cup mayonnaise or salad dressing
    ½ teaspoon salt
      dash pepper
    1½ cups chopped cabbage
    ½ cup shredded carrot
    ½ cup shredded sharp process American cheese
      dash celery seed

Dissolve gelatin in boiling water; add vinegar.
Combine mayonnaise or salad dressing, salt, and
pepper; gradually add gelatin mixture. Chill until
partially set. Combine chopped cabbage, carrot,
cheese, and celery seed. Fold into gelatin mixture.
Pour into six to eight ½-cup molds. Chill until
firm. Unmold the salads on lettuce-lined plates.
Makes 6 to 8 servings.

SAUERKRAUT AND APPLE SALAD

    1 can (16 ounce) sauerkraut, rinsed and drained
    1 cup diced apple
    1 small onion, chopped
    ¼ cup finely chopped celery
    1 cup grated carrots
    ¼ cup chopped parsley
    3 tablespoons vegetable oil
    1 tablespoon cider vinegar
    ¼ teaspoon salt
      dash pepper
    1½ teaspoons sugar
      Lettuce

Toss sauerkraut, apple, carrots, onion, celery and
parsley together in a bowl. Measure oil, vinegar, salt,
pepper and sugar into a cup or small bowl. Use a wire
whisk to blend thoroughly. Pour over sauerkraut mixture;
mix lightly. Cover; refrigerate 30 minutes. Spoon
salad mixture onto lettuce leaf. Serves 5.

BANANA-CARROT SALAD

2 medium bananas, sliced
2 cups shredded carrots
1 can (20 ounce) pineapple chunks in syrup, drained
¼ cup raisins
  Cottage-Cheese Dressing
  Lettuce

In bowl combine bananas, carrots, pineapple and
raisins. Add dressing; toss lightly. Chill
well. Spoon into lettuce-lined bowl. Makes 4
servings.

COTTAGE-CHEESE DRESSING

 1 cup cottage cheese
   reserved pineapple syrup

In blender, mix until smooth. Makes 1-1/3 cups.

FRENCH FRIED POTATO SALAD

1 16-ounce package frozen french fried potatoes
½ cup Russian salad dressing
 1 cup sliced celery
½ cup sliced radishes
 1 cup sour cream dip with French onion
2 tablespoons milk
1 tablespoon snipped parsley
1 tablespoon lemon juice
½ teaspoon salt

In skillet, combine frozen potatoes and Russian
dressing. Cook over low heat until defrosted.
Cover and heat 2 to 4 minutes, stirring gently
once or twice. Pour into mixing bowl. Combine
remaining ingredients; stir into potatoes. Chill
well. Makes 6 servings.

GOLDEN CARROTS VINAIGRETTE

8 to 10 large carrots
4 green onions with part of tops, chopped
2 tablespoons chopped parsley
2 tablespoons grated lemon peel
½ cup oil
3 tablespoons lemon juice
¼ teaspoon dry mustard
½ teaspoon salt
¼ teaspoon white pepper

Peel carrots and cut in matchsticks or slice diagonally 1/8 inch thick. Cook covered in about 1 inch boiling water about 5 minutes or until crisp-tender. Drain; plunge into cold water. Drain again; place in serving bowl. Mix in green onions, parsley and lemon peel. In small bowl whisk oil, lemon juice, mustard, salt and pepper. Pour over carrots and toss to coat. Cover and chill. Makes about 8 servings.

CONFETTI PEA SALAD

1 cup fresh peas
½ teaspoon salt
3 hard-cooked eggs, chopped
½ cup chopped celery
½ cup coarsely grated carrot
¼ cup sweet pickle relish
1 tablespoon chopped onion
½ cup mayonnaise or salad dressing
½ cup (2 ounces) shredded process American cheese
1 teaspoon salad seasoning
1 teaspoon prepared mustard

In large bowl, gently toss together peas, eggs, celery, carrot, pickle relish, and onion. Combine mayonnaise, cheese, salad seasoning, and mustard; toss with vegetable mixture. Cover and chill. Makes 4 servings.

SUNSHINE SUMMER SALAD

4 cups mixed greens
1 cup celery, thinly sliced
1 cup zucchini, cut lengthwise in half, then thinly
  sliced
1 cup cucumber, cut length wise in half (seeds
  removed), then thinly sliced
¼ pound mushrooms, thinly sliced
1 large tomato, diced
½ cup parsley, coarsely chopped
2 tablespoons grated Parmesan
2 tablespoons pumpkin seeds
1 tablespoon sunflower seeds
1 tablespoon sliced almonds
4 radishes, sliced
½ cup Tofu or Yogurt Dressing
1 cup cottage cheese
1 cup grated raw beets
1 cup grated carrots
1 cup alfalfa sprouts

Toss together all ingredients except cottage cheese,
beets, carrots and sprouts. Serve mixture on four
salad plates. Top each with ¼ cup cottage cheese
and surround with ¼ cup beets, carrots and sprouts.
Garnish with lemon wedge and parsley sprigs. Makes
4 servings.

MARINATED VEGETABLES ITALIANO

3 medium potatoes
1 cup tomato wedges
2 cups broccoli flowerets
1 cup mushroom slices
½ pound asparagus spears, cooked, drained
1 8-ounce bottle Italian Dressing
    lettuce

Cook, peel and slice potatoes. Combine with tomatoes,
broccoli, mushrooms and asparagus. Pour dressing
over vegetables. Cover; marinate in refrigerator
overnight. Drain, reserving marinade. Arrange
vegetables on lettuce-covered platter. Serve with
reserved marinade. Garnish with celery leaves.
Makes 6 servings.

SOUTH-OF-THE-BORDER POTATO SALAD

4 medium potatoes
½ cup salad oil
¼ cup vinegar
1 tablespoon sugar
1½ teaspoon chili powder
1 teaspoon seasoned salt
    dash hot pepper sauce
1 small onion, thinly sliced and separated into rings
1 8-ounce can whole kernel corn, drained
½ cup shredded carrot
½ cup chopped green pepper
½ cup sliced pitted ripe olives

Cook potatoes in boiling salted water until tender,
about 35 to 40 minutes. Drain, pare, and cube.
Combine oil, vinegar, sugar, chili powder, seasoned
salt, and hot pepper sauce. Add to warm potatoes;
toss gently to coat. Cover and chill 1 hour. Fold
in remaining ingredients. Garnish with additional
halved ripe olives. Serve chilled. Makes 6 to 8
servings.

WALDORF COLESLAW

3 cups grated carrots
3 cups shredded cabbage
2 cups chopped apples
½ cup raisins
¼ cup peanuts
   Salad Dressing or mayonnaise

Combine cabbage, apples, raisins, nuts and enough
salad dressing to moisten. Toss lightly. Makes
8 to 10 servings.

TANGY HAM-POTATO SALAD MOLD

2 pounds potatoes
½ cup vegetable oil
3 tablespoons vinegar
1 tablespoon prepared mustard
1 teaspoon salt
¼ teaspoon pepper
1 large green pepper
1 pound cooked ham, diced
1 cup diced celery
1 small onion, chopped
1 cup dairy sour cream
3 hard-cooked eggs, chopped
   lettuce leaves

Cook potatoes in boiling salted water until tender,
about 25 minutes. Drain; peel and cut into ½ inch
cubes to make 4 cups. Combine oil, vinegar, mustard,
salt and pepper in a large bowl. Add warm potatoes;
toss lightly. Let stand at room temperature 20
minutes. Cut pepper in half crosswise; seed. Slice
half the pepper into rings for garnish; reserve.
Cut remaining half in ¼-inch strips and dice. Add
diced green pepper, ham, celery, onion, sour cream
and eggs; mix well. Press into a 4-quart mold or
large round bowl. Cover and refrigerate 2 hours or
overnight. Unmold onto a round platter over lettuce
leaves. Garnish with reserved green pepper rings.
Makes 8 servings.

SIDE DISHES

BRANDIED CANDIED SWEET POTATOES

½ cup butter or margarine
½ cup packed brown sugar
¼ cup brandy
½ teaspoon salt
3 cans (17 to 18 oz. each) sweet potatoes, drained

Melt butter in large skillet. Stir in sugar, brandy
and salt until sugar dissolves. Add potatoes;
stir over low heat until potatoes are well glazed
and heated through. Makes 12 servings.

CHEEZY POTATOES

4 cups mashed potatoes
2 cups grated cheddar cheese
4 green onions, chopped
4 strips bacon, cooked crisp and crumbled

Fold in 1 cup cheese, onions and bacon into
mashed potatoes. Top with leftover cheese.
Bake for 20 minutes at 350°.

CARROT AND APPLE TZIMMES

4 cups grated carrots
1 tablespoon fine barley
1 cup grated apples
3 tablespoons butter
½ cup water
½ teaspoon salt
2 teaspoons sugar
¼ teaspoon nutmeg

Combine all ingredients in saucepan. Cover and
cook over low heat 2 hours, or until the barley
is soft. Serves 6.

CHEESE-STUFFED BAKED POTATOES

8 large baking potatoes
½ cup milk
¼ cup butter or margarine
½ cup sour cream
1 cup tiny cubes of Swiss cheese
1½ teaspoons salt
¼ teaspoon pepper
¼ cup shredded Swiss cheese

Scrub potatoes well; pat dry. Prick skins with a fork. Place potatoes in a large shallow pan. Bake at 425° for 55 minutes or until potatoes are soft. Cut thin lengthwise slice from top of each potato. Carefully scoop out insides with a spoon, leaving a ¼-inch shell; place in large bowl. Return shells to pan. Combine milk and butter in a small saucepan; heat slowly until butter melts. Mash potatoes; beat in hot milk mixture until potatoes are fluffy. Stir in sour cream, Swiss cheese cubes, salt and pepper. Spoon back into shells, mounding slightly. Re-bake potatoes at 350° for 25 minutes; top each potato with some of the shredded Swiss cheese; bake an additional 5 minutes or until lightly browned.

CARROTS OREGANO

1 pound, quartered carrots
   salt to taste
2 tablespoons water
3 tablespoons butter
½ teaspoon oregano

Place carrots in shallow 1-quart baking dish. Add remaining ingredients. Cover, bake at 350° for 45-60 minutes.

VEGETABLE MEDLEY

¼ cup butter
3 cups thick-sliced parsnips
1 cup carrot sticks or chunks
1 medium-sized onion, sliced
1 teaspoon dill weed
   salt to taste
1 teaspoon chicken bouillon granules
   fresh pea pods or snap peas

Melt butter in saucepan. Toss vegetables, except
pea pods, and seasoning with butter. Cover and
cook over medium heat until vegetables are tender-
crisp. Stir in pea pods. Continue cooking until
parsnips are tender. Makes 6 servings.

CARROTS POLYNESIAN

1 cup water
1 teaspoon salt
2 cups thinly sliced carrots
1 can (8 ounces) crushed pineapple
1 tablespoon cornstarch blended with
2 tablespoons water
1 cup celery, diagonally sliced
½ cup blanched almonds
   juice of ½ orange

Bring water and salt to boil in medium saucepan.
Add carrots and celery, cover and cook 10 minutes
until crisp-tender. Stir in pineapple and juice
of orange; cook 5 minutes. Add cornstarch mixture.
Cook and stir until thickened and clear, about 2
minutes. Sprinkle almonds on top before serving.
Makes 4 servings.

CARROT TZIMMES

5 large carrots
5 medium white potatoes
3 medium sweet potatoes
2½ to 3 pounds beef brisket
1 teaspoon salt
½ cup sugar
  water
1 small onion (optional)
2 tablespoons flour browned with
2 tablespoons chicken fat or vegetable shortening

Peel and cut carrots into thin rounds. Peel and cut white potatoes into quarters. Peel and cut sweet potatoes into 1-inch thick rounds. Sear the brisket of beef in pot to be used for cooking, turning frequently until evenly browned. Add the vegetables, salt and sugar. Add enough water to cover all ingredients about 1-inch. Keep this amount of water in pot until meat is tender. Cook over low heat after bringing to a boil. Do not stir. If an onion is used, it should be left whole, with one or two cuts in the bottom to permit the flow of juice. Remove before it becomes too mushy. When the liquid has been reduced to half, pour into a casserole. Add thickening (flour browned with chicken fat). Shake the casserole to distribute the thickening. Bake at 350° for 30 minutes or until brown on top.

COMPANY CARROTS

4 cups fresh sliced carrots
1 cup sour cream
1 (3 ounce) package cream cheese
3 tablespoons finely chopped green pepper
2 tablespoons chopped green onion
½ teaspoon salt
½ teaspoon grated lemon peel

Cook carrots 10 minutes; drain. Combine all other
ingredients in sauce pan. Stir over low heat
until blended, do not boil. Add carrots and heat
thoroughly. Serves 6.

SAVORY VEGETABLES

16 cauliflorets
16 finger broccoli florets
16 snow peas
 2 carrots, thinly sliced
 1 cup fresh peas
 4 to 6 tablespoons butter
 1 chicken bouillon cube, crumbled
   black pepper

Steam vegetables, except for peas, for 5 minutes.
Melt butter in large frying pan. Add 1 crumbled
bouillon cube and stir into butter. Add vegetables,
including peas, and toss over a medium heat until
tender. Season with black pepper and serve.
Makes 4 servings.

BRAISED CARROTS AND ZUCCHINI

4 carrots, cut into chunks
3 small zucchini, cut into chunks
1 small onion, chopped
2 tablespoons butter
  water
  salt and pepper to taste

Cook carrots in boiling salted water for about 15
minutes; add zucchini for last 5 minutes. Drain.
Lightly brown carrots, zucchini and onion in butter.
Add 3/4 cup water and season with salt and pepper.
Cover and cook until vegetables are tender. Uncover,
to evaporate liquid. Sprinkle with chopped parsley.
Makes 4 servings.

CARROT SOUFFLE

3 medium carrots
3 tablespoons butter or margarine
3 tablespoons all-purpose flour
1 cup milk
½ teaspoon salt
4 eggs, separated

Scrape and dice or slice carrots and cook in boiling
salted water until just tender. Drain and mash.
Measure 1 generous cup of pulp. Melt butter in skillet
Stir in flour, blending thoroughly. Slowly stir in
milk, a little at a time. Cook over low heat,
stirring constantly, until smooth and thickened. Add
salt and let mixture cool slightly. Beat egg yolks
until light and lemon-colored; add to cooled mixture.
Add carrot pulp and blend. Beat egg whites until
stiff but not dry. Fold half of beaten whites into
carrot mixture thoroughly. Add remaining whites and
fold in gently. Butter a 2-quart souffle dish and
fill with mixture. Bake at 375º for 30 to 40 minutes,
or until souffle is puffed and lightly browned. Makes
4 servings.

GNOCCHI

2 pounds potatoes, boiled and peeled
1½ cup flour
 1 egg
   tomatoe sauce or meat sauce

Sieve potatoes; let the resulting puree cool, then
add flour and egg. Mix well. When flour and
potatoe are blended, roll into little rolls ¼-inch
in diameter each; cut them into one-inch lengths.
With a twist of the thumbs, open them a little
in the middle. Let them stand on a linen
cloth. Place gnocchi in large pot of boiling
salted water. Take out of water when they float
to the top. Top with tomato sauce or meat sauce
and grated parmesan cheese. Serves 6.

SWEET POTATO CASSEROLE

2¼ pounds sweet potatoes, cooked and pared
 6 tablespoons butter or margarine
 3 slightly beaten eggs
 ½ cup sugar
 ½ cup chopped pecans
 ½ cup flaked coconut
 ½ cup orange juice
 ½ teaspoon salt
 ½ teaspoon vanilla
10 orange slices
10 marshmallows

Mash potatoes; stir in butter or margarine. Beat
in eggs, sugar, pecans, coconut, orange juice, salt
and vanilla. Pour into 1½-quart casserole. Bake,
uncovered, for 30 minutes at 350°. Top with
orange slices; place one marshmallow on top of each
orange slice. Return to oven until marshmallows
are golden brown. Makes 8 to 10 servings.

SAUCY HAM AND POTATO BAKE

2 tablespoons chopped onion
¼ cup butter
¼ cup flour
1 teaspoon salt
½ teaspoon dry mustard
  dash pepper
2 tablespoons chopped pimento
1½ cups milk
2 cups shredded Cheddar cheese
½ pound ham cut into 1/8-inch slices
6 cups cooked potato slices

Saute onion in butter. Blend in flour and seasonings.
Gradually add milk; cook stirring constantly until
thickened. Toss potatoes in cheese sauce. Pour
into 2-quart casserole, reserving 1 cup potato slices.
Arrange ham and remaining potato slices on top of
casserole. Bake at 350°, 30 minutes. Top with
remaining cheese. Makes 6 servings.

VEGETABLE CHOLENT

1 pound dried lima beans
  water
3 large onions, sliced
2 cloves garlic, crushed
3 tablespoons oil
4 potatoes, peeled and quartered
1 tablespoon salt
2 teaspoons paprika
½ teaspoon pepper, or to taste
1 bay leaf
  boiling water

In large saucepan cover beans with water and soak
overnight; or bring to boil, cook 2 minutes, cover,
remove from heat and let stand 1 hour. Drain; set
aside. In Dutch oven saute onions and garlic in oil
until tender. Add beans, potatoes, salt, paprika,
pepper and bay leaf. Add boiling water to cover
completely; mix well. Cover tight and bake at 250°
for 6 to 8 hours. Discard bay leaf. Makes 6 servings

THREE VEGETABLE CASSEROLE

1 9-ounce package frozen green beans
1 9-ounce package frozen peas and carrots
1 3½-ounce can French fried onions
1 tablespoon chopped green pepper
1 tablespoon chopped pimiento
2 cups milk
6 tablespoons butter
4 slices white bread
½ teaspoon salt
3 eggs, beaten
  shredded cheddar cheese

Cook beans and peas and carrots according to
package directions. Drain and combine with half
the onions, green pepper and pimiento in a well-
greased 9-inch square baking dish. Scald the
milk with ¼ cup butter. Cut bread in cubes, after
removing crust. Add bread cubes, salt and eggs.
Mix well. Pour over vegetables. Sprinkle with
cheese and 2 tablespoons butter. Bake at 350°
for 45 minutes or until custard is set. Remove
from oven and sprinkle with remaining onions.
Bake 5 minutes longer. Makes 6 to 8 servings.

CREAMED CUCUMBERS AND CARROTS

2 large cucumbers
2 cups cooked carrot rounds
3 tablespoons butter
3 tablespoons flour
1½ cups milk
¼ cup chopped parsley
  Paprika

Split cucumbers lengthwise; remove seeds. Dice cucumbers
boil in small amount of salted water for 15 minutes.
Melt butter; stir in flour. Add milk gradually; cook,
stirring constantly, until thick. Combine carrots,
drained cucumbers and sauce; add parsley. Sprinkle
paprika over top; serve. Makes 8 servings.

CREAMED CARROTS AND ZUCCHINI

2 small unpeeled zucchini, sliced
8 baby carrots
2 tablespoons butter
2 tablespoons all-purpose flour
3 tablespoons nonfat dry milk

Cook carrots in boiling salted water for about 15
minutes; add zucchini for last 5 minutes. Drain;
reserving liquid. Melt butter in saucepan; remove
from heat and stir in flour. Mix nonfat dry milk
with enough carrot/zucchini liquid to make 1 cup milk.
Add to saucepan. Return to heat. Cook over low heat,
stirring constantly, until thickened. Add carrots
and zucchini and heat a little longer. Makes 4 to
6 servings.

SPICED APRICOT SWEETS

1 can apricot halves (1-pound 1-ounce)
   whole cloves
1½ pounds sweet potatoes, cooked, peeled and
   quartered
1 tablespoon sugar
1 tablespoon butter

Drain syrup from apricots into a 2-quart saucepan;
add 3 whole cloves. Boil until reduced to 1/3 cup,
about 8 to 10 minutes. Place half the sweet
potatoes on bottom of 1½-quart casserole; top with
half the apricots. Repeat layers. Stick a clove
into each apricot half in the top layer. Pour
reduced syrup over all; sprinkle with sugar and
dot with butter. Bake at 350° for 30 minutes.
Makes 6 servings.

SWEET POTATO PECAN STUFFING

4 cups mashed, cooked sweet potatoes or yams
2 cups butter or margarine, melted
3 cups finely chopped onion
2 cups finely chopped celery
2 cups coarsely chopped pecans
1½ teaspoons salt
1½ teaspoons dried thyme leaves
1½ teaspoons dried marjoram leaves
½ teaspoon dried sage
¼ teaspoon pepper
8 cups toasted bread cubes

In large bowl mash sweet potatoes until smooth;
beat in 1 cup butter. In remaining hot butter
saute onion and celery, in large skillet, stirring
until onion is golden. Add to potato, along with
pecans, salt, thyme, marjoram, sage and pepper;
mix well. Add bread cubes and mix well. Cool
before using. Makes 10 cups, enough for a 12
pound turkey.

POTATO-CHEESE PIE

3 eggs
1 teaspoon salt
½ teaspoon rosemary or nutmeg
¼ teaspoon pepper
2 cups half-and-half
4 medium potatoes, peeled and shredded coarse
¼ cup sliced green onions, including tops
1 cup coarsely shredded sharp Cheddar cheese

Beat eggs, salt, rosemary and pepper until well
blended. Stir in half-and-half, potatoes and
onions. Turn into well greased 8-inch square
baking pan. Sprinkle with cheese. Bake at
400° for 35 to 40 minutes or until knife inserted
in center comes out clean and potatoes are tender.
Cool for 5 minutes. Cut in squares to serve.
Makes 4 servings.

SOUTHERN PEACH YAM BAKE

½ cup packed brown sugar
3 tablespoons flour
½ teaspoon nutmeg
2 tablespoons margarine
½ cup chopped pecans
2 (17-oz.) cans yams, drained
1 (16-oz.) can peach slices, drained
1½ cups miniature marshmallows

Combine sugar, flour and nutmeg; cut in margarine
until mixture resembles coarse crumbs. Add nuts.
Arrange yams and peaches in 1½ quart casserole;
sprinkle with sugar mixture. Bake at 350º for
35 minutes. Sprinkle with marshmallows. Broil
until lightly browned. Serves 6.

MASHED POTATO STUFFING

10 medium potatoes
 1 tablespoon salt
 ½ cup butter or margarine
 1 cup chopped onion
 ½ cup chopped celery
 4 cups toasted bread crumbs
 2 teaspoons salt
 1 teaspoon sage
 1 teaspoon dried thyme leaves
 3 eggs, beaten

Pare potatoes; quarter. Boil in large saucepan
with 1 tablespoon salt about 20 minutes, or until
tender. Drain well; return to saucepan. Mash
potatoes until smooth. Heat slowly over low
heat, stirring, to dry out about 5 minutes.
In hot butter in medium skillet, saute onion and
celery 5 minutes or until tender. Add mashed
potato to onion-celery mixture, along with
bread crumbs, salt, sage and thyme. Mix well.
Beat in eggs. Makes 10 cups, enough for a 12
pound turkey.

BANANA SWEET POTATOES

6 medium sweet potatoes
1 cup mashed banana
¼ cup butter or margarine, softened
½ teaspoon finely shredded lemon peel
½ teaspoon salt
2 egg yolks
2 stiff-beaten egg whites

In large saucepan cook sweet potatoes in boiling
salted water for 30 to 40 minutes or until tender;
drain. Peel potatoes; mash. Add banana, butter
or margarine, lemon peel, and salt. Beat until
fluffy. Add yolks; beat well. Fold in stiff-
beaten egg whites. Pour into 1½ quart casserole.
Bake covered, at 350⁰ for 20 minutes; uncover
and bake 25 minutes. Serves 8 to 10.

GRATED-POTATO TZIMMES

1 pound unsweetened prunes
3 cups water
8 potatoes, peeled
½ cup brown sugar
2 tablespoons lemon juice
1½ teaspoons salt
3 tablespoons potato flour
2 tablespoons melted fat
   dash pepper

Wash prunes and soak in water 1 hour. Bring to
boil. Slice five potatoes into a 2-quart
casserole and pour the undrained prunes over them.
Add the brown sugar, lemon juice and 1 teaspoon
salt. Cover and bake for 1 hour at 350⁰. Grate
the remaining potatoes and add the potato flour,
fat, pepper and remaining salt. Spread the mixture
over the top of the casserole. Replace cover and
bake another 1¼ hours, removing the cover for the
last 45 minutes. Serve 6 to 8.

FRESH VEGETABLE MEDLEY

4 new potatoes, peeled
2 cups vegetable, beef or chicken bouillon, divided
3 medium carrots, halved lengthwise and cut in
   2" pieces
¼ pound snap beans, cut in ½" pieces
½ cup celery in 1½" pieces
2 tomatoes, halved
1 tablespoon margarine

Put potatoes in saucepan with 1 cup bouillon and
bring to a boil. Cook, uncovered 5 minutes, then
cover and simmer 15 minutes, or until tender. In
another saucepan, cook carrots and beans in
remaining bouillon, uncovered, 5 minutes. Cover
and cook 5 minutes longer. Add celery and cook
5 minutes. Meanwhile, dot tomato halves with the
margarine. Broil to desired doneness. Arrange
tomatoes on serving plate and surround with drained
vegetables. Makes 4 servings.

ALMOND VEGETABLES MANDARIN

1 cup thinly sliced carrots
1 cup green beans cut about 1-inch
2 tablespoons salad oil
1 cup thinly sliced cauliflower
½ cup sliced green onion
1 cup water
2 teaspoons chicken stock base
2 teaspoons cornstarch
   pinch garlic powder
½ cup unblanced whole almonds

Cook and stir carrots and beans with oil in large
skillet over medium high heat 2 minutes. Add
cauliflower and onion; cook 1 minute longer. Add mix
of water, chicken stock base, cornstarch and garlic.
Cook and stir until thickened. Vegetables should
be crisp-tender. Add almonds. Makes 4 to 6 servings.

GLAZED MINTED CARROTS

1½ pounds carrots, peeled and quartered
1½ cups water
3½ tablespoons butter
½ teaspoon salt
1 cup heavy cream
2 tablespoons sugar
    black pepper to taste
2 tablespoons chopped fresh mint

In large skillet combine carrots with water, 1½
tablespoons butter and salt; heat to boiling.
cover and cook slowly until liquid has evaporated
and carrots are almost tender, about 20 minutes.
In small saucepan heat cream to boiling and pour
over the carrots. Simmer slowly, uncovered, until
cream has been almost absorbed by carrots or until
carrots are tender. Add remaining 2 tablespoons
butter, sugar and pepper. Simmer a few minutes
longer. Add chopped mint and serve. Makes 6
to 8 servings.

SUMMER SQUASH CASSEROLE

2 pounds yellow summer squash, sliced
¼ cup chopped onion
1 can condensed cream of chicken soup
1 cup dairy sour cream
1 cup shredded carrot
1 8-ounce package herb-seasoned stuffing mix
½ cup butter, melted

In saucepan, cook sliced squash and chopped onion
in boiling salted water for 5 minutes; drain.
Combine cream of chicken soup and sour cream.
Stir in shredded carrot. Fold in drained squash
and onion. Combine stuffing mix and butter.
Spread half of stuffing mixture in bottom of
12x7½x2-inch baking dish. Spoon vegetable mixture
on top. Sprinkle remaining stuffing over vegetables.
Bake at 350° for 25 to 30 minutes. Makes 6 servings.

MASHED RUTABAGAS AND CARROTS

3½ pounds rutabagas
1 pound carrots
3¼ teaspoons salt
   dash pepper
½ cup butter or margarine, melted

Wash rutabagas; pare. Cut into quarters and slice
1-inch thick. Pare carrots; cut in half crosswise.
In a 5-quart dutch oven, combine rutabagas and carrots
with water to cover and add 2 teaspoons salt. Bring
to boil, reduce heat, cover and simmer 40 minutes
or until tender. Drain well. Return vegetables
to saucepan; beat until smooth, adding rest of
salt, pepper and butter or margarine. Serves 8.

VEGETABLE SCRABBLE

3 quarts water
6 cups peeled and diced carrots
1 tablespoon salt
3 cups peeled and chopped potatoes
½ cup butter
1 large onion, chopped
2½ cups shredded sharp Cheddar cheese
3 tablespoons chopped parsley
1½ teaspoons salt
   dash pepper

Grease 2-quart casserole; set aside. In large
saucepan place water, carrots and salt. Cover;
bring to boil over medium heat and cook 10 minutes.
Add potatoes; cook 10 to 15 minutes more until
vegetables are tender. Remove from heat; drain.
In same saucepan, mash carrots and potatoes until
smooth. Cover and keep warm; set aside. Meanwhile,
in small skillet melt butter over low heat. Add
onion and saute until tender, about 3 to 5 minutes.
Add to mashed potatoes-carrots with remaining
ingredients. Spoon into prepared casserole. Bake
at 375° for 45 minutes. Makes 8 servings.

SAUCY CARROTS WITH WATER CHESTNUTS

1 pound carrots, peeled and sliced ½-inch thick
2 tablespoons butter
1 8-ounce can water chestnuts, drained and sliced thin
1 teaspoon dried thyme, crushed
¼ teaspoon ground ginger
3 tablespoons dry white wine
1 tablespoon snipped parsley

In a covered saucepan cook carrots in a small
amount of boiling salted water for 15 to 20
minutes or until crisp-tender. Drain and set
aside. In saucepan melt butter; add water
chestnuts, thyme, and ginger. Cook and stir for
2 minutes. Add wine, parsley, and cooked carrots;
cook and stir until heated through. Makes 6 to
8 servings.

POTATO LATKES

3 medium potatoes, peeled and shredded
1 egg
¼ cup grated onion, drained
2 tablespoons flour
½ teaspoon salt
  dash pepper
  oil
  sour cream, applesauce, or preserves

Place potatoes in colander; press down to extract
as much liquid as possible. In medium bowl,
lightly beat egg with onion. Stir in flour,
salt and pepper. Add potatoes. In large skillet
heat ½-inch oil to 350°. Spoon tablespoons of
potato mixture into hot oil a few inches apart.
Flatten each to about 2½-inch diameter circle.
Fry until golden brown, turning once. Drain.
Keep warm in 200° oven. Serve with sour cream,
applesauce or preserves. Makes 20.

WISCONSIN FARM MASHED POTATOES/CARROTS

6 medium potatoes
2 medium carrots
6 slices bacon, including drippings
  dash garlic powder
  salt and pepper to taste

Cook potatoes and carrots together until done;
drain, reserving some of the water. Fry bacon
until crisp and drain. Crumble. Mash potatoes
and carrots together adding a little of the water
and a healthy portion of the bacon grease to get
consistency and flavor desired. Mix in crumbled
bacon. Makes 6 to 8 servings.

MISSISSIPPI SWEET POTATOES

12 small sweet potatoes
 1 cup sugar
 1 cup packed brown sugar
 1 teaspoon ground cinnamon
 1 tablespoon fresh lemon juice
 1 cup melted butter
 1 teaspoon salt

Peel sweet potatoes and leave whole. Put potatoes
in a shallow greased baking dish. Mix remaining
ingredients and cook at a boil for 8 minutes.
Pour hot syrup over potatoes and bake at 350° for
1 hour, or until syrup is thick and potatoes are
tender. Spoon syrup in dish over potatoes several
times during cooking. Makes 6 servings.

MAIN DISHES

HAM-STEAK, SWEET-POTATO AND PRUNE SKILLET

1 fully cooked ham steak (1 pound)
1 tablespoon oil
½ cup orange juice
½ cup packed brown sugar
1½ teaspoons cider vinegar
1 teaspoon dry mustard
¼ teaspoon ginger
1 can (17 ounces) sweet potatoes, drained
½ cup pitted prunes

In large skillet fry ham in oil, turning once, 10
to 12 minutes or until heated through. Remove to
serving platter; keep warm. In same skillet mix
well juice, sugar, vinegar, mustard and ginger. Add
potatoes and prunes. Cook and stir gently until all
is mixed well and heated through. Serve potatoes and
prunes with ham; top with pan juices. Makes 4 servings.

TURKEY-MUSHROOM QUICHE

1 cup finely chopped cooked turkey
1 3-ounce can sliced mushrooms, drained
1 cup grated carrots
1 9-inch baked pastry shell, cooled
1 cup shredded process American cheese
1 can condensed cream of shrimp soup
¼ cup milk
4 slightly beaten eggs

Arrange turkey, mushrooms and carrots in prepared
pastry shell; sprinkle with cheese. In small
saucepan, combine soup and milk; heat just to
boiling, stirring constantly. Gradually stir
into eggs. Pour soup mixture over cheese. Bake
at 325° for 40 to 45 minutes or until knife
inserted in center comes out clean. Let stand
10 minutes. Makes 6 servings.

SPRINGTIME SPAGHETTI

1 cup thinly sliced carrots
½ pound each; asparagus, green beans, zucchini
  cut into 1-inch pieces
1 cup fresh peas
½ cup broccoli flowerettes
  salt and pepper to taste
¼ pound prosciutto or ham, diced
8 leaves basil, chopped
1 teaspoon dillweed
¼ cup olive oil
1 cup red pepper, diced
1 pound spaghetti, cooked just until tender
3 cloves crushed garlic
½ cup scallions, thinly sliced

Steam the first six ingredients for five minutes.
Set aside. Saute garlic in oil until golden. Add
scallions, red pepper, and cook for five minutes
longer, stirring. Add steamed vegetables, prosciutto,
basil, and cook until mixture is heated through but
still crunchy. Season with salt and pepper to taste.
Toss the primavera mixture with drained pasta. Serve
immediately. Serves 4.

SKILLET PORK-CHOP SUPPER

4 pork chops about 3/4 inch thick
1 can (10-3/4 ounces) condensed tomato soup
½ cup water
1 bell pepper, quartered
6 to 8 small unpeeled whole potatoes or 3 medium
  potatoes, quartered
4 small carrots, cut in 2-inch lengths
1 teaspoon Worcestershire
½ teaspoon each salt and caraway seed

Brown chops in large skillet. Pour off drippings.
Stir in soup, water, potatoes, carrots, bell pepper,
Worcestershire, salt and caraway seed. Cover and
simmer 45 minutes or until chops are tender. Makes
4 servings.

NEW ENGLAND TUNA PIE

2 pie crust doughs
1 can (7 ounces) chunky light tuna
3 large potatoes, pared and thinly sliced
2 large onions, thinly sliced
2 tablespoons butter
2 tablespoons chopped parsley
1½ teaspoons salt
¼ teaspoon pepper
   Creamy Pea Sauce

Roll half the pastry on a lightly floured board
to a 12-inch round. Fit into a 9-inch pie plate.
Flake tuna into pie plate; layer potato and onion
slices over tuna, dotting each layer with part of
the butter and seasoning with part of the parsley,
salt and pepper. Roll out remaining pastry to an
11-inch round; cut some slits in center of pastry;
transfer to top of pie; turn under rim and flute
edge. Bake at 400° for 55 minutes or until pastry
is golden and potato slices are tender. Cut into
wedges and serve with Creamy Pea Sauce.

CREAMY PEA SAUCE

Melt ¼ cup butter in medium saucepan; stir in
¼ cup all-purpose flour, 1 teaspoon salt and ¼
teaspoon ground allspice and cook 1 minute; stir
in 1-3/4 cups skim milk; cook, stirring constantly,
until sauce thickens and bubbles 3 minutes; add 1
package (10 ounces) frozen peas, cooked and drained.
Serve hot over wedges of New England Tuna Pie.
Makes 6 servings.

WHOLE WHEAT VEGETARIAN PIE

1 cup whole wheat flour
1 cup all-purpose flour
1 cup shortening
5 to 7 tablespoons cold water
1 cup chopped zucchini
½ cup chopped celery
1 cup shredded carrot
½ cup sliced fresh mushrooms
½ cup chopped green pepper
1 clove garlic, minced
2 tablespoons cooking oil
1 (15-ounce) can tomato sauce
½ cup cooked cut green beans
½ cup cooked whole kernel corn
1 tablespoon brown sugar
1 teaspoon dried oregano, crushed
1 teaspoon chili powder
½ teaspoon salt
½ teaspoon dried basil, crushed
¼ teaspoon pepper
¼ teaspoon ground allspice
1 cup shredded Cheddar cheese
1 beaten egg

Stir together flours and 1 teaspoon salt. Cut in
shortening until pieces are the size of small peas.
Sprinkle water, 1 tablespoon at a time, tossing
mixture after each addition. Form into ball. Roll
half of the pastry to 1/8-inch thickness. Fit into
a 9-inch pie plate. Trim. In a skillet cook
zucchini, celery, carrot, mushrooms, green pepper,
and garlic, covered, in hot oil until tender. Add
tomato sauce, beans, corn, sugar, and seasonings.
Simmer, uncovered, 5 minutes. Spoon into pie shell.
Sprinkle with cheese. Roll out remaining pastry.
Adjust top crust; seal edge and crimp. Cut vents
in top pastry. Beat egg and 1 tablespoon water
together. Brush over crust. Cover edges with foil.
Bake at 350° for 20 minutes. Remove foil. Bake for
20 to 25 minutes. Let stand 10 minutes before serving.
Makes 6 servings.

NEW ENGLAND BOILED DINNER

3 to 4 pounds corned brisket of beef
3 to 4 pounds cross ribs of beef
1 piece salt pork
2 bay leaves
6 peppercorns
1 chicken
6 large carrots, scraped
6 medium onions, peeled
6 large potatoes, peeled
6 parsnips
6 medium turnips, peeled
1 head of cabbage, quartered
2 medium beets quartered and cooked

Wipe corned beef with a damp cloth; tie it into
shape and place in a large stock pot or heavy
bottomed casserole. Add cold water to cover and
bring slowly to boil. Drain and rinse beef. Repeat
this procedure. Drain. Place prepared corned beef
in a large stock pot; add cross ribs of beef, salt
pork, bay leaves and peppercorns. Add boiling
water to cover. Bring to boil, skimming surface
of liquid occasionally. Then, cover pot and simmer
over very low heat for 3 hours or until meat is
tender. Add chicken after the first 1½ hours.
Cool slightly; skim off excess fat and add carrots,
onions, potatoes, parsnips and turnips. Cook for
about 20 minutes, then add cabbage wedges; cook
until cabbage and vegetables are crisp and tender.
Serve meats and chicken on a platter garnished with
vegetables and cooked beets. Accompany with mustard
or horseradish sauce and pickles. Makes 8 to 12
servings.

BOEUF EN DAUBE (MEDITERRANEAN-STYLE BEEF STEW)

2 cups dry red wine
1 medium onion, chopped
2 cloves garlic, minced
1 tablespoon vinegar
1 teaspoon salt
¼ teaspoon pepper
½ teaspoon dried rosemary, crushed
½ teaspoon dried thyme, crushed
½ teaspoon finely shredded orange peel
2 to 2½ pounds beef stew meat, cut in 1-inch cubes
2 ounces salt pork
½ cup beef broth
6 carrots, bias-cut in 1-inch pieces
3 onions, quartered
1 cup pitted ripe olives
2 tablespoons cornstarch
2 tablespoons cold water

Combine wine, chopped onion, garlic, vinegar, salt, pepper, rosemary, thyme and orange peel. Add beef; stir to coat. Cover and marinate at room temperature for 2 hours. Drain meat, reserving marinade; pat meat dry with paper towel. In 4-quart Dutch oven, cook salt pork until there are 2 to 3 tablespoons fat; discard pork. Brown meat in the hot fat. Add marinade and broth; bring to boiling. Cover; simmer 1 hour. Add vegetables and olives; simmer, covered, 30 to 40 minutes. Blend cornstarch and water; add to pot. Cook and stir until bubbly. Turn into bowl; top with parsley. Serves 8 to 10.

BEEF-POTATO LOAF

1 medium onion, chopped fine
1 medium clove garlic, minced
2 tablespoons butter
1 pound lean ground beef
½ cup fine dry bread crumbs
½ cup water
1 egg
1 teaspoon each, oregano and salt
½ cup minced green onions with tops
1¼ cups cold well-seasoned firm mashed potatoes

Brown chopped onion and garlic in butter until
golden and tender, stirring occasionally. Cool.
In mixing bowl combine beef, bread crumbs, water,
egg, oregano, salt and browned onion-garlic mixture.
Blend well with hands. Rinse a 12-inch long piece
of wax paper with cold water. With wet hand flatten
meat mixture on paper to form a 9x8 rectantle.
Sprinkle with half the green onions. With hand,
flatten mashed potatoes on top to within ½ inch from
edge and sprinkle with remaining green onions.
Starting at long side and with help of waxed paper,
roll up jelly-roll fashion and shape into smooth
loaf. Put seam side down in greased 9x5x3-inch
loaf pan. Bake at 350° for 1 hour or until done.
Cool and chill. Unmold and slice. Makes 6 servings.

WACKY STEWED CHICKEN

1 whole chicken (3 pounds), trimmed of visible fat
1 teaspoon salt
½ teaspoon rosemary, crushed
¼ teaspoon pepper
1 can (10-3/4 ounces) condensed cream of chicken
  soup, undiluted
3 carrots
3 medium onions
3 large potatoes

(CONTINUED)

81

Sprinkle chicken with ½ teaspoon salt, rosemary and pepper; rub seasonings into the skin. Put the chicken into a 2½-3 quart casserole dish with a cover. Spoon the chicken soup over the chicken. Cover the casserole dish and bake at 375º for 40 minutes. Peel the carrots and chop into 1-inch pieces. Peel the onions and cut each one into quarters; set aside. Peel the potatoes and chop into pieces about the same size as the carrots; set aside. At the end of 40 minutes, remove casserole from oven; set aside. Add carrots, onions and potatoes to casserole. Sprinkle with ½ teaspoon salt. Cover and return to 375º oven for 45 minutes more, until vegetables are tender when pierced with a fork. Remove from oven and skim off any fat that forms with a spoon. Makes 4 servings.

NEW ENGLAND-STYLE PLATTER

2 (12 ounce) cans beer
2 cups water
½ cup chopped onion
2 cloves garlic, minced
2 bay leaves
9 peppercorns
4 medium or 2 large carrots, peeled and cut into sticks
4 medium potatoes, peeled and cut up
6 smoked pork chops, cut 1-inch thick
6 cabbage wedges
4 tablespoons packed brown sugar
2 tablespoons horseradish mustard

In a Dutch oven combine beer, water, onion, garlic, bay leaves, and peppercorns. Add potatoes and carrots; cover and bring to a boil. Reduce heat and simmer, covered, 15 minutes. Add pork chops and cabbage wedges atop vegetables, pushing them into the cooking liquid. Cover and simmer 15 to 20 minutes more until cabbage is done and chops are heated through. Season to taste with salt and pepper. Blend brown sugar and mustard. To serve, place drained pork chops and vegetables on warm platter. Serve with brown sugar mixture. Makes 6 servings.

TURKEY MADRAS

¼ cup butter
2 small onions, chopped
1 clove garlic, finely chopped
1 stalk celery, diced
3 carrots, finely chopped
1 tart apple, pared and diced
2 tablespoons flour
1 teaspoon curry powder
1 teaspoon salt
½ teaspoon dry mustard
   dash sage
1 can (13-3/4 ounces) chicken broth
1 bay leaf
3 cups cut-up cooked turkey or chicken
½ cup light cream
2 tablespoons chopped chutney
3 cups hot cooked rice

Melt butter in saucepan. Saute onions, garlic,
celery, carrots and apple about 5 minutes or
until tender. Remove from heat. Mix in flour,
curry powder, salt, mustard and sage. Cook over
low heat, stirring constantly, until mixture is
bubbly, 1 minute. Stir in broth; add bay leaf.
Cook, stirring constantly, until thickened and
bubbly. Stir in turkey, cream and chutney; heat
through. Remove bay leaf. Press rice lightly
in well buttered 4-cup ring mold. Keep hot
until serving time. Invert ring on platter.
Fill center with turkey mixture. Makes 6 servings.

CHICKEN WITH WALNUT SAUCE

5 quarts water
2 carrots, halved lengthwise
1 medium onion
1 celery stalk with some leaves
3 sprigs parsley
1 teaspoon salt
¼ teaspoon pepper
1 roasting chicken (4 to 5 pounds)
3 slices white bread, crusts removed
2 cups walnuts
1 clove garlic, crushed
1 teaspoon grated lemon peel
1 tablespoon lemon juice
1 tablespoon each paprika and minced parsley

Bring water to boil in large pot. Add carrots,
onion, celery, parsley sprigs, salt and pepper.
Carefully lower chicken, breast side up, into
water. Bring again to boil, cover and cook over
medium heat 30 minutes. Remove from heat and
refrigerate at once (do not lift cover). Allow
chicken to cool in broth about 3 hours or until
sides of pot are cool to touch. Remove chicken and
strain broth, reserving ½ cup for sauce. Discard
skin and slice breast meat thin; cut off remaining
meat in large chunks. Arrange on platter, cover
and set aside. Tear bread in pieces into blender.
Pour in reserved broth and blend at high speed
until well blended. Add walnuts ½ cup at a time,
blending at high speed and scraping container.
Add garlic, lemon peel and juice and blend again.
Spread each piece of chicken generously with
sauce. Sprinkle with paprika and minced parsley.
Makes 4 to 6 servings.

STUFFED VEAL ROLL

1 boned breast of veal (2½ to 3 pounds)
2 teaspoons salt
¼ teaspoon pepper
½ pound bulk sausage
4 ounces mozzarella cheese, shredded
2 hard-cooked eggs, chopped fine
2 cloves garlic, minced
3 tablespoons finely chopped parsley
¼ teaspoon leaf oregano, crumbled
2 tablespoons olive or vegetable oil
1 cup grated carrot
1 cup chopped onion
1 bay leaf
½ cup white wine
½ cup water

Spread breast of veal flat on a cutting board.
Pound with wooden mallet to even out. Sprinkle
both sides with salt and pepper. Combine sausage
meat, mozzarella, eggs, garlic, parsley and oregano in
a small bowl; combine thoroughly. Pressing firmly,
shape into an oblong in center of meat, leaving
1 inch at each end of veal. Roll up veal from long
side, jelly-roll fashion. Tie crosswise with
heavy string at 1½ inch intervals. Brown meat in
oil in Dutch oven; add carrots, onions, bay leaf, wine
and water. Bake, covered at 350° for 2 hours, or
until meat is tender. Remove meat to cutting board.
Put pan juices and vegetables into a large bowl.
Remove bay leaf. Remove excess fat from juices.
Pour pan juices into blender; cover; puree until
smooth. Pour into small saucepan; heat. Remove
string from veal; cut into thin slices; serve
with vegetable sauce. Makes 6 servings.

CROWN ROAST OF PORK

16 rib crown roast of pork
   salt, pepper, ginger, garlic powder
   Sweet potato puff
16 cherry tomatoes, or browned mushroom caps

Season roast on all sides with salt, pepper, plus
dash of ginger and garlic powder. Place in a
shallow roasting pan. Cover tips of rib bones with
aluminum foil, to prevent excess browning. Roast
at 350º for about 1½ hours. Remove from oven,
fill cavity with Sweet Potato Puff, baking excess in
greased casserole. Transfer to serving platter and
remove foil. Cut thin slice from stem end of each
tomato, press to remove seeds, and center a tomato
(or mushroom cap), cut side down, on each rib end.
Cut between ribs to serve. Spoon out potato
filling. Makes 8 to 16 servings.

SWEET POTATO PUFF

6 cups cooked or canned sweet potatoes
6 tablespoons butter, melted
1 tablespoon brown sugar
   salt, pepper, nutmeg to taste
6 eggs, separated

Mash hot potatoes with butter and seasonings. Blend
in egg yolks. Beat egg whites stiff, fold into
potato mixture. Pile into center of Crown Roast,
and place remainder in greased casserole. Bake
at 350º about 40 minutes, until lightly puffed and
golden. Makes 12 servings.

THREE KINGDOM CHICKEN

1 whole chicken breast
1 cup uncooked medium-sized shrimp
2 tablespoons peanut or other salad oil
1 clove garlic, peeled and chopped fine
1 teaspoon peeled and finely chopped fresh gingerroot
1 scallion or green onion, chopped
1 cup thinly sliced raw tender beef (sirloin or flank)
1 tablespoon peanut or other salad oil
¼ cup sliced canned bamboo shoots
¼ cup sliced canned water chestnuts
¼ cup sliced celery
1 cup fresh or canned mushrooms, halved
1 cup sliced carrots
1 cup cold water
1 tablespoon soy sauce
2 tablespoons dry sherry wine
½ teaspoon sugar
1 teaspoon salt
  dash pepper
2 teaspoons cornstarch
2 tablespoons cold water
1 package (2½ ounces) blanched whole almonds, toasted

Rinse chicken breast and pat dry. Skin and bone
chicken breast and cut into 1-inch cubes. Shell
shrimp, devein and wash; split lengthwise, but do
not cut all the way through. Heat 2 tablespoons
oil in wok or skillet over high heat; add garlic,
ginger, scallion, chicken, shrimp, and beef; stir-
fry 1 minute and then turn out onto a plate. Heat
1 tablespoon oil in wok over high heat; add bamboo
shoots, water chestnuts, carrots, celery, mushrooms,
1 cup water, soy sauce, sherry, sugar, salt and
pepper and bring to a boil. Mix cornstarch with
2 tablespoons water; add to wok and cook 2 to 3 minutes,
stirring constantly, until thickened. Add chicken-
shrimp mixture and almonds and cook until well heated.
Makes 2 to 4 servings.

CHOUCROUTE GARNIE (GARNISHED SAUERKRAUT)

6 slices bacon, cut up
½ cup chopped onion
1 27-ounce can sauerkraut, drained
2 medium carrots, bias-sliced
1 tablespoon sugar
8 to 10 juniper berries (optional)
6 whole black peppercorns
2 whole cloves
1 bay leaf
1 large sprig parsley
1 cup chicken broth
½ cup dry white wine
4 potatoes, peeled and quartered
4 smoked pork chops
4 knockwurst, diagonally scored

In 12-inch skillet cook bacon and onion. Drain off
fat. Stir the sauerkraut, carrots and sugar into
skillet. Loosely tie juniper berries, pepper corns,
cloves, bay leaf, and parsley in cheesecloth bag;
bury in center of sauerkraut. Add broth and wine.
Bring to boiling. Reduce heat. Simmer, covered,
for 10 minutes. Add potatoes, pushing them into
sauerkraut. Simmer, covered, for 15 minutes. Top
with the meats; simmer, covered, 20 minutes. Discard
bag. Arrange sauerkraut and potatoes on platter.
Top with meats. Makes 4 to 6 servings.

VEGETABLE BEEF ROLLS

1 beaten egg
1½ pounds ground beef
½ cup shredded carrot
¼ cup finely chopped onion
¼ cup finely chopped green pepper
¼ cup finely chopped celery
½ teaspoon salt
   dash pepper
12 slices bacon
½ cup Italian salad dressing

Combine egg and ground beef; mix well. Divide
into six portions. On waxed paper, flatten each
meat portion into a 6x4 inch rectangle, ¼-inch
thick. Combine carrot, onion, green pepper, celery,
salt and pepper; divide and pat onto meat rectangles.
Roll up jelly-roll fashion. Wrap two slices bacon
around each roll and secure with toothpicks. Place
in shallow baking dish. Pour salad dressing over;
let stand at room temperature about 1 hour, reserving
marinade. Grill rolls over medium coals for 20 to 25
minutes, turning to grill all sides, brushing with
reserved dressing occasionally. Makes 6 servings.

CHICKEN SALTIMBOCCA

3 large chicken breasts, skinned, boned and halved
6 thin slices boiled ham
3 slices mozzarella cheese, halved
1 cup grated carrots
1 can chopped olives
½ teaspoon dried sage, crushed
½ cup fine dry bread crumbs
2 tablespoons grated parmesan cheese
2 tablespoons snipped parsley
4 tablespoons butter, melted

(CONTINUED)

89

Place chicken, boned side up, on cutting board.
Place a piece of clear plastic wrap over. Working
from the center out, pound lightly with meat mallet
to 5x5 inches. Remove wrap. Place ham slice and half
slice cheese on each cutlet. Top with carrots,
olives and a dash of sage. Tuck in sides; roll up
jelly-roll style, pressing to seal well. Combine
bread crumbs, parmesan and parsley. Dip chicken
into butter, then roll in crumbs. Place in shallow
baking dish. Bake at 350° for 40 to 45 minutes.
Serves 6.

GLAZED PORK KABOBS

½ cup apricot preserves
½ cup tomato sauce
¼ cup packed brown sugar
¼ cup dry red wine
2 tablespoons lemon juice
2 tablespoons cooking oil
1 teaspoon onion juice
1½ pounds lean boneless pork, cut in 1-inch pieces
4 large carrots, cut in 1-inch pieces and cooked
    fresh pineapple chunks

In saucepan, combine apricot preserves, tomato
sauce, brown sugar, wine, lemon juice, oil, and
onion juice. Boil, uncovered, 10 to 15 minutes.
Thread pieces of pork, carrot, and pineapple on
6 skewers; season with salt and pepper. Grill
and turn over medium coals 10 minutes. Brush with
apricot sauce; grill 5 minutes. Makes 6 servings.

CHICKEN BREASTS WITH PECAN-SAUSAGE STUFFING

1 pound pork-sausage meat
1 cup butter
2 cups sliced celery
½ cup grated carrot
1 large onion, chopped
1 cup chopped pecans
1 teaspoon salt
½ teaspoon savory leaves
¼ teaspoon fresh ground pepper
8 cups dried bread cubes
2 eggs beaten with 3 tablespoons milk
6 large chicken breasts, boned and split
  salt
  melted butter
  whole spiced crab apples
  parsley

In skillet saute meat until well browned; remove
from pan and set aside. Drain fat from skillet,
melt butter and saute celery and onion until tender.
Stir in pecans, salt, savory and pepper and saute 3
minutes longer. Stir in meat, then mix lightly
but thoroughly with bread cubes in large bowl.
Add egg mixture and toss until blended. Using
½-cup measure, form 12 mounds of stuffing and
arrange on foil-covered rack in large roasting
pan. Sprinkle meat side of breasts lightly
with salt; place 1 split breast, skin side up,
over each stuffing mound, tucking edges under to
form neat bundle. Brush tops generously with melted
butter and bake at 400° for 25 minutes, or until
golden brown. Arrange on platter with crab apples
and parsley. Makes 12 servings.

PASTIES

2 cups sifted all-purpose flour
½ teaspoon salt
½ teaspoon baking powder
2 cups shortening
  cold water
  Meat Filling
  butter

Sift flour with salt and baking powder. Add
shortening and cut into flour until tiny particles
are formed. Add enough cold water to make a dough the
consistency of pie crust. Chill. Roll out dough
to 1/8-inch thickness on a lightly floured board.
Cut out eight 7-inch rounds. Divide Meat Filling into
8 portions and cover half of each round with the
mixture. Dot top of Filling with butter. Fold
pastry over Meat Filling and seal by moistening
edges. Lift with a spatula and put on a cookie
sheet. Bake at 350° for 1 hour, or until pastry
is golden brown. Makes 8 pasties.

MEAT FILLING

Mix together 1½ pounds hamburger; 3 cups finely diced
potatoes, 1 cup sliced onions; 1 teaspoon salt and
¼ teaspoon pepper.

SPICY SZECHUAN SHREDDED BEEF AND VEGETABLES

2 tablespoons finely minced fresh ginger root
1 clove garlic, crushed
¼ teaspoon ground cloves
¼ teaspoon ground cinnamon
  dash fennel seeds, crushed
  dash anise seeds, crushed
¼ teaspoon crushed dried red chili peppers
3 tablespoons soy sauce
3 tablespoons dry sherry
1 tablespoon vegetable oil
1 pound boneless top round
3 tablespoons vegetable oil
3 medium-size carrots, finely shredded
3 medium-size celery ribs, thinly sliced
8 green onions, thinly sliced
  hot cooked rice

Combine ginger, garlic, cloves, cinnamon, fennel,
anise, chili peppers, soy, sherry and 1 tablespoon oil
in a jar with a screw-top lid. Shake marinade well
to mix. Cut beef in very thin strips about the size
and shape of shoe-string potatoes. Put beef strips
in large bowl. Shake marinade again and pour over
beef; toss; let stand at room temperature for 1
hour, turning once or twice. Heat 2 tablespoons
oil in a wok or large skillet; add carrots, celery and
green onions. Stir-fry about 3 minutes or just
until crisp-tender. Quickly add remaining tablespoon
of oil, the beef and any remaining marinade. Stir-
fry 3 minutes longer or until beef is no longer
bright red. Serve with hot cooked rice. Makes
6 servings.

FARMERS' OMELET

1 package (5.5 ounces) hash brown potatoes with onion
3 cups boiling water
3½ tablespoons butter
½ cup chopped green pepper
½ cup chopped onion
½ teaspoon salt
  dash pepper
6 eggs, slightly beaten
3 tablespoons sour cream
½ cup shredded Cheddar cheese
  dash bottled red pepper sauce

Place potatoes in bowl. Add boiling water and let
stand 15 minutes. Drain well. In a heavy skillet,
melt butter. Add potatoes and cook until lightly
brown. Add green pepper and onion. Continue to
cook until onion and pepper are tender. Season with
salt and pepper. In small bowl, combine eggs, sour
cream, cheese and pepper sauce. Mix lightly. Pour
egg mixture into buttered 10-inch skillet. As
omelet cooks, lift it with a spatula to allow the
uncooked part to run under. Increase heat slightly
to brown underside, when omelet is of desired doneness.
Makes 4 servings.

STIR-FRY CHICKEN WINGS

1 pound chicken wings
½ teaspoon salt
1 bunch green onions
2 large carrots
2 red peppers
2 tablespoons vegetable oil
1 cup thinly sliced celery
1 cup frozen peas
3 tablespoons water
  Sweet-Sour Sauce
3 cups cooked rice

(CONTINUED)

Cut chicken wings at each joint to separate.
Sprinkle salt in a large heavy skillet; heat; add
chicken wings and brown about 5 minutes on each side;
remove and reserve. Trim green onions and cut with
tops into 2-inch pieces; pare carrots and cut into
long, diagonal pieces; seed peppers and cut into
long strips. Add oil to skillet; stir-fry onions,
carrots and peppers in oil; add chicken wings, celery,
frozen peas and water; cover skillet and let steam
15 minutes; add Sweet and Sour Sauce and cook 3
minutes. Serve with hot rice. Serves 6.

SWEET-SOUR SAUCE

Combine 1/3 cup firmly packed brown sugar and
4 teaspoons cornstarch in a small saucepan; stir
in 1 cup water, 1 teaspoon or envelope instant
chicken broth, 3 tablespoons cider vinegar and
3 tablespoons soy sauce. Bring to boiling, stirring
constantly; let bubble 2 minutes. Makes 1½ cups.

OLD ENGLISH MEAT PIE

1 pound beef liver
¼ cup all-purpose flour
1 teaspoon salt
¼ teaspoon pepper
¼ cup vegetable oil
4 large carrots
2 large potatoes
2 large onions, sliced
    water
2 envelopes or teaspoons instant beef broth
1 teaspoon leaf sage or thyme, crumbled
1 single pastry dough crust

Cut beef liver into 1½-inch squares; coat with a
mixture of flour, salt and pepper. Brown beef
liver, part at a time, in hot oil in a large skillet;
remove to an 8-cup casserole. Pare and slice carrots
and potatoes; cook in salted boiling water 10
minutes, or just until tender; reserve cooking liquid.
Saute onions in drippings in skillet until soft.
Add water to vegetable cooking liquid to make 2 cups;
stir into skillet with beef broth and sage or thyme.
Cook, stirring constantly, until sauce thickens and
bubbles; pour over vegetables and liver in casserole.
Roll out pastry to a round 1-inch wider than the
diameter of casserole; make slits in pastry to allow
steam to escape. Transfer pastry to top of casserole,
turning under pastry around edge and fluting. Bake
at 400° 40 minutes, or until pastry is golden brown.
Makes 6 servings.

SKILLET COQ AU VIN

½ cup all-purpose flour
1 teaspoon salt
¼ teaspoon pepper
3 to 3½ pound broiler-fry chicken, cut up
6 slices bacon
6 small onions
8 ounces mushrooms, sliced
½ teaspoon dried thyme leaves
1 bay leaf
2 large sprigs parsley
4 carrots, halved
1 teaspoon instant chicken bouillon (or 2 cubes)
1 cup hot water
1 cup red Burgundy
1 clove garlic, crushed
½ teaspoon salt

Mix flour, 1 teaspoon salt and the pepper; coat
chicken with flour mixture. Fry bacon in large
skillet until crisp; remove bacon from skillet
and drain. Brown chicken in bacon fat over
medium heat. Remove chicken from skillet; reserve.
Cook and stir onions and mushrooms in skillet until
mushrooms are tender, about 5 minutes. Drain off
fat. Tie thyme leaves, bay leaf and parsley in
cheesecloth or place in tea ball. Crumble bacon;
stir bacon, herbs in cheesecloth and remaining
ingredients into skillet. Add reserved chicken and
cover. Simmer until done, about 1 hour. Remove
cheesecloth. Spoon off fat. Serve in individual
bowls. Garnish with sprigs of parsley.

CHICKEN FRICASSEE WITH DUMPLINGS

3 pounds chicken parts (legs, thighs, breasts, wings)
½ cup flour
1½ teaspoons salt
1 teaspoon dried marjoram leaves
¼ cup butter
2 medium onions, sliced
1 cup chopped celery
6 large carrots, pared and halved
1 bay leaf
4 whole cloves
9 whole black peppers
1 can (13-3/4 ounces) chicken broth

DUMPLINGS

1½ cups packaged biscuit mix
   snipped chives or chopped parsley
1 egg
¼ cup milk
½ cup light cream

Wash chicken; pat dry. On waxed paper, combine
flour with salt and marjoram; mix well. Coat
chicken with flour mixture, evenly. Shake off excess.
Reserve 2 tablespoons left over flour. Saute chicken
in 2 tablespoons hot butter in 6-quart Dutch oven
until browned on all sides, about 15 minutes. To
drippings, add onion, celery, carrots, bay leaf,
cloves and black peppers; saute stirring 5 minutes.
Stir in broth and 1 cup water; bring to boil.
Return chicken to Dutch oven. Bring to boil; reduce
heat; simmer, covered, 40 minutes. In medium bowl,
combine biscuit mix and 2 tablespoons chives; with fork
blend in egg and milk. Drop batter by 6 rounded
tablespoonfuls, 2 to 3 inches apart, onto chicken
(not in liquid). Cook, uncovered, over low heat 10
minutes. Cover tightly; cook 10 minutes, or until
dumplings are light and fluffy. Remove dumplings
to baking dish; keep warm in low oven. In small
bowl, combine reserved flour mixture with the light

(CONTINUED)

(CHICKEN FRICASSEE WITH DUMPLINGS CONTINUED)

cream, stirring until smooth. Stir flour mixture
gently into fricasse; simmer 5 minutes, or until
mixture is thickened. Replace dumplings on top
of fricasse to serve. Reheat gently, covered, until
hot. Before serving, sprinkle with more chives or
parsley. Makes 6 servings.

TIVOLI MEAT RING

1 pound ground beef
½ pound ground veal
½ pound ground pork
2 eggs
1 cup mashed potatoes
1 medium onion, finely chopped
1 cup sour cream
2½ teaspoons salt
1 teaspoon dill weed
¼ teaspoon pepper
1 can (16 ounce) whole cranberry sauce
   boiled new potatoes and green peas

Grease a 6½-cup ring mold or 9x5-inch loaf pan.
Combine all ingredients except cranberries, potatoes
and peas, in a large mixing bowl. Stir until well
mixed. Spoon into ring mold or pan. Bake at 350°
for 40 to 45 minutes for ring mold and 55 minutes for
loaf pan. Remove from oven. Drain off excess liquid.
Invert onto a jelly-roll pan; remove pan. Top with
berries and return to oven. Continue baking for 15
minutes. Transfer to heated platter. Serve
immediately with boiled new potatoes and green peas.
Makes 8 servings.

BAKED CORNED BEEF BURGERS

1 slightly beaten egg
1 cup soft bread crumbs
¼ cup mayonnaise or salad dressing
½ cup finely chopped green pepper
½ cup finely chopped onion
1 12-ounce can corned beef, finely flaked
½ cup fine dry bread crumbs
2 tablespoons cooking oil
1 can condensed cream of celery soup
1 8½ ounce can carrots
1 teaspoon horseradish mustard
½ cup milk
3 slices sharp process American cheese, halved diagonal
3 English muffins, split and toasted

In mixing bowl, combine egg, the soft bread crumbs,
mayonnaise, green pepper, onion, and a dash pepper.
Stir in corned beef; mix well. Using about 1/3 cup
mixture for each, shape into 6 patties. Coat with
dry bread crumbs. In skillet, cook patties in
hot oil 2 to 3 minutes on each side. Combine soup,
carrots, and mustard. Gradually add milk, stirring
until smooth. Spoon half the soup mixture over
bottom of 12x7½x2 inch baking dish. Arrange patties
over sauce. Spoon on remaining sauce. Bake,
uncovered, in 400° oven for 15 to 20 minutes. Place
a cheese triangle over each patty. Bake 3 to 5 minutes
more. Serve over English muffin halves. Makes 6
servings.

DESSERT

CHRISTMAS PUDDING

1 cup grated carrots
1 cup grated potatoes
1 teaspoon soda
½ teaspoon nutmeg and cloves
1 teaspoon cinnamon
1 cup raisins and sugar
1 cup suet or butter
  Flour enough to hold stiff

Mix all ingredients and pour into 1 pound coffee
can. Steam for 3 hours.

MAE'S CHOCOLATE CAKE

1½ cups sugar
 ½ cup shortening
 3 unbeaten eggs
 2 cups flour
 ¼ teaspoon salt
 1 teaspoon soda
 3 squares unsweetened chocolate, melted and cooled
 1 cup sour or butter milk
 1 teaspoon vanilla
 ½ cup nuts
 1 cup mashed potatoes

Combine all ingredients, mix well. Pour into
13x9x2-inch pan. Bake at 350° for 45 minutes.
Frost with peppermint frosting when cooled.

PEPPERMINT FROSTING

In top part of small double boiler combine 2 egg
whites, 1½ cups sugar, dash salt, 1/3 cup water, and
2 teaspoons light corn syrup. Put over boiling
water and beat with rotary beater for 7 minutes or
until mixture will stand in stiff peaks. Add ½
teaspoon peppermint extract. Spread on cooled
cake.

14 KARAT CAKE

2 cups flour
2 teaspoons baking powder
1½ teaspoon soda
2 teaspoons cinnamon
1 teaspoon salt
2 cups brown sugar
1½ cups oil
4 eggs
2 cups grated raw carrots
1 (8½ ounce) crushed pineapple
1 cup walnuts

Sift together flour, baking powder, soda,
cinnamon and salt. Add brown sugar, oil and
eggs and mix well. Stir in carrots, pineapple and
walnuts. Bake in 13x9x2-inch pan at 350° for
35 to 40 minutes.

FROSTING:

Cream ½ cup butter, 8 ounces cream cheese, 1 teaspoon
vanilla and 1 pound powdered sugar. Add small
amount of milk if needed to get to desired consistency.

NUTTY CHOCOLATE CANDY COOKIES

1½ cups semisweet chocolate pieces
4 tablespoons butter
1 cup sugar
1 egg
1½ teaspoons vanilla
1 cup carrots, finely grated
½ cup all-purpose flour
½ teaspoon salt
¼ teaspoon baking powder
½ cup chopped walnuts

(CONTINUED)

(NUTTY CHOCOLATE CANDY COOKIES CONTINUED)

In small saucepan over low heat, melt 1 cup of
the chocolate pieces; cool. In smaller mixer bowl,
cream together butter and sugar; add egg and vanilla.
Beat well. Blend in melted chocolate. Thoroughly
stir together flour, salt and baking powder. Add to
creamed mixture, mixing well. Stir in walnuts,
carrots and remaining ½ cup chocolate pieces. Drop
dough from teaspoon two inches apart onto lightly
greased cookie sheet. Bake at 350° for 8 to 10
minutes. Makes about 2½ dozen cookies.

RUM-WALNUT PIE

1½ cups pureed sweet potato
1 cup packed brown sugar
1 teaspoon ground cinnamon
½ teaspoon ground ginger
½ teaspoon ground nutmeg
3 eggs
1 cup evaporated milk
3 tablespoons dark rum
1 cup chopped walnuts
½ cup whipping cream
2 teaspoons granulated sugar
1 9-inch pie crust, unbaked

In bowl combine sweet potato, brown sugar, cinnamon,
½ teaspoon salt, ginger and nutmeg. Lightly beat
eggs into mixture. Stir in evaporated milk and rum;
mix well. Stir in nuts. Place pie plate on oven rack;
pour sweet potato mixture into shell. Bake at 375°
for 45 to 50 minutes or until knife inserted in
center comes out clean. Cool. Beat cream with
granulated sugar to soft peaks. Spoon on top of
cool pie and serve.

CARROT-RAISIN PIE

1 cup shredded carrots
2 cups seeded raisins
1 cup water
½ cup corn syrup
¼ cup lemon juice
¼ cup cornstarch
¼ teaspoon salt
  pastry for 1-crust, 10-inch pie and lattice
  topping, unbaked

Wash raisins; drain. Add water and carrots; simmer
for 10 minutes. Add corn syrup mixed with cornstarch
and salt; cook for 3 minutes, stirring constantly.
Cool; pour into pastry-lined pie pan; arrange strips
of pastry over top. Bake at 425° for about 20 minutes
Makes 6 servings.

BLONDE BROWNIES

1 cup sifted all-purpose flour
½ teaspoon baking powder
1 cup mashed potatoes
  dash baking soda
½ teaspoon salt
½ cup butter
1 cup firmly packed brown sugar
1 egg, lightly beaten
1 teaspoon vanilla
½ cup coarsely chopped walnuts
1 package (6 ounces) semisweet chocolate pieces

Sift flour, baking powder, baking soda and salt onto
wax paper. Melt butter in small saucepan; stir in
brown sugar. Pour into a large bowl; cool. Stir
in egg and vanilla. Beat in the dry ingredients.
Stir in the walnuts and half of the chocolate pieces.
Spread batter into a greased 9x9x2 inch pan.
Sprinkle batter with remaining chocolate pieces,
pressing in slightly. Bake at 350° for 20 minutes
or until mixture starts to pull away from edge
of pan. Cool in pan; cut into squares. Makes
about 36 squares.

RED VELVET CAKE

1 cup butter
1½ cup sugar
2 eggs
2 ounces red food coloring
1 teaspoon vanilla
2 tablespoons cocoa
1 teaspoon salt
1 cup mashed potatoes
1 cup buttermilk
2½ cups sifted flour
1 tablespoon vinegar
1 teaspoon soda

Cream butter, sugar and eggs. Make paste with food coloring and cocoa; add to butter mixture. Add salt, buttermilk, flour, potatoes and vanilla. Add soda to vinegar and mix entire batter. Do not beat hard. Bake at 350° for 30 minutes. Cool.

ICING:

5 tablespoons flour
1 cup milk
1 cup sugar
1 cup butter
1 teaspoon vanilla

Cook flour and milk until thick; cool. Cream butter and sugar until fluffy; add vanilla and cooled flour and milk mixture. Mix well.

CARROT PUDDING

1 cup coarse dried bread crumbs
1 cup firmly packed light brown sugar
½ cup all-purpose flour
1 teaspoon each of baking powder and baking soda
1 teaspoon salt
1 teaspoon ground cinnamon
½ teaspoon each of ground allspice and nutmeg
1 egg
½ cup diced candied orange peel
1 cup golden raisins
1 cup grated scraped raw carrot
1 cup grated peeled raw potato
1 cup chopped peeled tart apple
½ cup butter

Combine all ingredients in order given; mix well.
Pack into greased 1½-quart pudding mold. Cover and
steam for 4 hours, or until done. Serve warm, topped
with hard sauce and a few strips of candied orange
peel, if desired. Makes 8 to 10 servings.

POTATO CHIP COOKIES

2 cups sweet potatoes, cooked and mashed
4 teaspoons baking powder
2 teaspoons soda
1 teaspoon salt
2 teaspoon cinnamon
4 cups flour
2 cups sugar
2 beaten eggs
2 tablespoons milk
1 cup vegetable oil
2 teaspoons vanilla
1 (6 ounce) package butter-scotch chips
1 cup nuts

Mix all ingredients. Drop by teaspoonsful on a
cookie sheet and bake at 375º for 14 minutes.
Makes about 10 dozen.

CARROT-ORANGE COOKIES

1 cup shortening
1 cup sugar
1 egg, unbeaten
1 cup mashed cooked carrots
1 teaspoon vanilla extract
2 cups sifted all-purpose flour
2 teaspoons baking powder
½ teaspoon salt
  Orange Frosting

Cream shortening until light and fluffy. Gradually
beat in sugar. Add egg, carrots, and vanilla;
beat well after each addition. Sift together dry
ingredients and combine with carrot mixture. Mix well.
Drop batter by tablespoonfuls onto greased cookie
sheets. Bake at 350° for about 20 minutes. Cool.
Frost with Orange Frosting while still warm. Makes
about 4 dozen.

ORANGE FROSTING

Combine juice of ½ orange, grated rind of 1 orange,
1 tablespoon butter, and 1 cup sifted confectioners
sugar.

CARROT BROWNIES

½ cup butter
1½ cups firmly packed light brown sugar
 2 cups unsifted all-purpose flour
 2 teaspoons baking powder
 ½ teaspoon salt
 2 eggs
 2 cups finely grated carrots
 ½ cup chopped walnuts
   Cream Cheese Frosting
   Walnut halves

   (CONTINUED)

Melt butter in large saucepan. Add brown sugar; stir until blended. Remove from heat; cool slightly. Sift flour, baking powder and salt onto wax paper. Beat eggs into cooled butter mixture one at a time. Stir in flour mixture, blending well. Add carrots and walnuts, mixing well. Pour into two greased 8x8x2 inch baking pans. Bake at 350° for 30 minutes or until center springs back when lightly pressed with fingertip. Cool 10 minutes on wire rack; remove from pans; cool completely. Frost tops with Cream Cheese Frosting. Cut into squares and top each square with a walnut half. Makes 32 squares.

CREAM CHEESE FROSTING

Combine 2 ounces softened cream cheese with 1/3 cup softened butter in a small bowl; beat until smooth. Stir in 1 teaspoon vanilla and 1½ cups confectioners' sugar until fluffy and smooth. Makes 1 cup.

CARROT TORTE

4 eggs, separated
1 cup sugar
1 cup grated raw carrot
  grated rind of 1 lemon
  juice of ½ lemon
½ cup sifted all-purpose flour
1 teaspoon baking powder
¼ teaspoon salt
1 cup heavy cream, whipped

Beat yolks until thick and lemon-colored. Gradually beat in sugar, a few tablespoons at a time. Add carrot, lemon rind, and juice. Sift together dry ingredients and fold into yolk mixture. Beat egg whites until stiff but not dry and fold into first mixture. Pour into two ungreased 3-inch layer-cake pans. Bake at 350° for 25 to 30 minutes. Remove from oven and let stand in pan until cold. Remove from pan; spread sweetened whipped cream between layers and on top.

WHOLE WHEAT CARROT CAKE

1 cup cooking oil
1 cup granulated sugar
1 cup packed brown sugar
1 teaspoon vanilla
4 eggs
2 cups whole wheat flour
½ cup nonfat dry milk powder
1 teaspoon baking soda
1 teaspoon baking powder
2 teaspoons ground cinnamon
3 cups finely shredded carrots
1 cup chopped walnuts
  Broiled Coconut Topping

In large bowl blend oil, granulated sugar, and
brown sugar until well mixed. Add vanilla; beat
in eggs, one at a time, beating well after each
addition. In another bowl stir together flour,
milk powder, baking soda, baking powder, 1 teaspoon
salt, and cinnamon. Add to egg mixture until well
blended. Stir in carrots and walnuts. Pour batter
into well greased and floured 10-inch tube pan.
Bake at 350º for 50 to 60 minutes or until toothpick
inserted in center comes out clean. Cool in pan;
invert onto cookie sheet. Spread with Broiled
Coconut Topping.

BROILED COCONUT TOPPING

Combine 6 tablespoons butter, 2/3 cup firmly packed
brown sugar, ¼ cup heavy cream, 1 cup flaked
coconut and ½ teaspoon vanilla. Broil at least
4 inches from heat, until topping bubbles and turns
golden brown. Watch carefully to prevent scorching.
Cool.

WHITE POTATO PIE

1½ cups mashed cooked potatoes
½ cup butter
1 cup sugar
4 eggs
1 teaspoon lemon extract
3 tablespoons flour
½ cup evaporated or whole milk
   dash nutmeg
1 teaspoon vanilla
1 (9-inch) unbaked pie shell with ½ cup finely
   chopped nuts pressed in shell prior to filling

Mash or cream potatoes with butter. Add sugar, eggs,
flour and evaporated milk and beat 3 minutes until
smooth. Add nutmeg, vanilla and lemon extract. Turn
into pie shell and bake at 350° for 50 to 60
minutes, or until golden brown and firm on top.
Makes 6 to 8 servings.

SPICY SWEET-POTATO SQUARES

32 large marshmallows
 1 cup sweet potato, pureed
 ½ teaspoon ground cinnamon
 ¼ teaspoon ground ginger
   dash ground cloves
 1 cup crushed graham crackers
 ¼ cup butter, melted
 1 pint whipped cream, sweetened

In a large saucepan melt marshmallows with sweet
potatoes, cinnamon, ginger, and cloves over low
heat, stirring until smooth. Cool about 15 minutes.
Meanwhile, combine crushed graham crackers and
melted butter or margarine; reserve ¼ cup for topping.
Pat remaining crumbs firmly into bottom of an
8x8x2-inch baking dish. Fold whipped cream into
cooled marshmallow mixture. Spread marshmallow
mixture over crust. Sprinkle reserved crumbs
on top. Chill Several hours or overnight. Cut
into squares. Makes 12 servings.

OATMEAL SANDWICH

FILLING:

1 cup finely grated carrots
1 cup finely chopped dates
1 cup raisins
½ cup each dark corn syrup and boiling water
1 cup chopped walnuts

DOUGH:

2 cups flour
2 cups uncooked quick oats
1 teaspoon each baking powder and salt
½ teaspoon each cream of tartar and baking soda
1 cup butter or margarine, softened
1 cup packed brown sugar
2 eggs
½ cup sour cream

In small saucepan cook dates, raisins, corn syrup
and water until mixture reaches consistency of jam.
Remove from heat; stir in walnuts. Cool. Stir
together flour, oats, baking powder, salt, cream of
tartar and soda; set aside. In large bowl cream
butter, sugar and eggs. Blend in sour cream. Stir
in flour mixture until well blended. Spread half
the dough in well greased and floured 13x9x2-inch
baking pan. Evenly spread on filing. Spread
remaining dough evenly on top. Bake at 350º for
25 minutes or until well browned. Cool. Cut in
bars. Makes 36 bars.

SWEET-POTATO PUDDING

2 eggs
1 cup milk
2½ cups loosely packed coarsely grated peeled
   sweet potatoes
1 cup packed light brown sugar
1 teaspoon each ginger and cinnamon
¼ teaspoon salt
½ cup chopped walnuts
   whipped cream, lightly sweetened

In bowl with fork beat eggs until light. Add milk.
Stir in sweet potatoes, then sugar, ginger,
cinnamon and salt. Bake in greased round 1-½ quart
baking dish at 350° for 30 minutes. Sprinkle walnuts
around edge. Bake 30 to 40 minutes longer or until
slightly puffed and knife inserted in center comes
out clean. Cool Slightly. Spoon out and serve
warm with whipped cream. Serves 6 to 8.

HONEY-GLOW BARS

1½ cups flour
½ teaspoon salt
½ cup butter, softened
½ cup plus 2 tablespoons confectioners' sugar,
   divided
1 teaspoon lemon extract
1 cup grated raw potatoes
1 cup uncooked oats
½ cup honey

Stir together flour and salt; set aside. In large
bowl cream butter and ½ cup sugar until fluffy.
Add lemon extract. Add flour mixture and raw
potatoes. Stir in oats until blended. (Dough
will be quite stiff). Press into greased 11x7x2-inch
baking pan. Make wells in dough with back of spoon;
drizzle evenly with honey. Bake in preheated 325°
oven 25 to 30 minutes. Cool. Cut in 24 bars.
Sprinkle with remaining 2 tablespoons confectioners'
sugar.

CARROT PINEAPPLE CHIFFON PIE

4 medium carrots
1 cup sugar
½ cup bottled lemon juice
4 eggs, separated
2 envelopes unflavored gelatin
1 can (8 ounce) drained pineapple (reserve juice)
½ teaspoon salt
¼ teaspoon cream of tarter
1 cup whipped cream

Cook carrots in just enough water to cover with
¼ cup sugar, 1 tablespoon lemon juice. Drain.
Soften gelatin in pineapple juice on top of double
boiler. In blender place carrots, egg yolks,
balance of lemon juice and ¼ cup sugar. Blend
on low until pureed. Add carrot mixture and
pineapple to gelatin in double boiler. Cook over
boiling water until thickened. Cool. Beat egg
whites with ½ cup sugar & cream of tartar until
stiff but not dry. Fold meringue and whipped
cream into cooled carrot/pineapple mixture. Pour
into prepared Graham cracker crust. Chill for
at least 2 hours.

CARROT-APPLESAUCE CAKE

3 cups flour
3 teaspoons baking soda
1 teaspoon salt
3 teaspoons cinnamon
1 teaspoon nutmeg
4 eggs
1 cup oil
2 cups sugar
1 teaspoon vanilla
1 jar (15 ounces) applesauce
3 cups shredded carrots
1 cup raisins
1 cup chopped walnuts, divided

(CONTINUED)

In large bowl mix flour, baking soda, salt,
cinnamon and nutmeg; set aside. With whisk, beat
eggs. Stir in oil, sugar and vanilla. Add
applesauce and carrots; mix well. Add to flour
mixture, stirring just to moisten. Fold in raisins
and ½ cup walnuts. Pour into greased pan or pans.
Sprinkle with remaining walnuts. Bake at 350°
40 minutes or until toothpick inserted in center
comes out clean.

GOLDEN CHEESECAKE

1½ cups fine graham-cracker crumbs
½ cup butter or margarine, melted
2 envelopes unflavored gelatin
½ cup water
1 cup sugar
½ teaspoon salt
½ cup milk
3 eggs, separated
2 packages (8 ounces each) cream cheese
1¾ cups pureed cooked sweet potatoes
1 cup heavy cream
2 teaspoons vanilla extract
1 teaspoon grated orange rind

Mix crumbs and butter; reserve ¼ cup and press
remainder onto bottom of 9-inch pan. Chill.
Soften gelatin in cold water in top part of a small
double boiler. Add ½ cup sugar, salt, milk, and
slightly beaten egg yolks. Cook, stirring constantly,
over boiling water until slightly thickened. Pour
over cheese and potatoes; beat until smooth and
blended. Cool. Beat egg whites until foamy; add
¼ cup sugar and beat until stiff. Whip cream and
fold into first mixture with egg whites. Add
flavorings. Pour into prepared pan. Sprinkle with
remaining crumbs. Chill until firm.

114